Sovereignty and the Status Quo

Sovereignty and the Status Quo

The Historical Roots of China's Hong Kong Policy

Kevin P. Lane

Westview Press
BOULDER, SAN FRANCISCO, & OXFORD

Westview Special Studies on China and East Asia

This Westview softcover edition is printed on acid-free paper and bound in library-quality, coated covers that carry the highest rating of the National Association of State Textbook Administrators, in consultation with the Association of American Publishers and the Book Manufacturers' Institute.

Published in 1990 in the United States of America by Westview Press, Inc., 5500 Central Avenue, Boulder, Colorado 80301, and in the United Kingdom by Westview Press, Inc., 36 Lonsdale Road, Summertown, Oxford OX2 7EW

Library of Congress Cataloging-in-Publication Data
Lane, Kevin.
   Sovereignty and the status quo: the historical roots of China's
Hong Kong policy/Kevin P. Lane.
      p. cm.—(Westview special studies on China and East Asia)
   Includes bibliographical references.
   ISBN 0-8133-7681-5 (lib. bdg.)
   1. Hong Kong—History. 2. Hong Kong—Politics and government.
I. Title. II. Series.
DS796.H757L36 1990
951.25—dc20   89-78301
                                                                            CIP

Printed and bound in the United States of America

The paper used in this publication meets the requirements
of the American National Standard for Permanence of Paper
for Printed Library Materials Z39.48-1984.

10   9   8   7   6   5   4   3   2   1

For John V. and Patricia M. Lane

Contents

Foreword

This book is a "must" for all interested in Hong Kong. Lane's excellent analysis of its past and present provides invaluable background for considering its future.

To speculate about this future one must at least start with understanding the facts about Hong Kong's survival hitherto. Lane sets these out selectively and readably, and he successfully avoids confusing the facts with his conclusions from them—which show great insight.

I hope the contents of this book will be studied. They record the decades of patience, compromise and mutual restraint that have permitted Hong Kong's remarkable success. Readers may find surprising the degree of flexibility that China has contributed to this process and may reflect on what has been done and not done by the British that has assisted.

Lane believes that on historical track record China has the capacity for flexibility on Hong Kong that would enable arrangements about its future to work successfully; if this may not be conclusive, it is encouraging.

Lord MacLehose
former governor of Hong Kong
Beoch, Scotland

Acknowledgments

In the course of researching and writing this book, I have depended heavily on the support and assistance of others. Dartmouth College's James B. Reynolds Scholarship provided generous financial support for my research in Hong Kong. At Dartmouth, Susan Blader, Charles MacLane, Hua-yuan Li Mowry and Laurence Radway were inspirational teachers who provided crucial advice and encouragement during the initial stage of research.

At The Chinese University of Hong Kong, Kuan Hsin-chi was a patient teacher and insightful critic who gave generously of his time, even when the project lasted much longer than he probably had expected. Peter Lee was both friend and teacher, making me feel at home in Hong Kong and offering perceptive comments on the manuscript. The administration and staff of the International Asian Studies Programme at Chinese University were extremely helpful in facilitating my research in Hong Kong. Terry Lautz, Thomas Lee and Mark Sheldon welcomed me into the university community and opened many doors that helped make the research possible. Josephine Mak and Fannie Chow patiently answered my daily questions about how to get around Hong Kong and gave me frequent help with the Cantonese dialect. The librarians and staff at Chinese University and the University of Hong Kong libraries provided professional and efficient assistance, as did the staff at Chinese University's computer center.

At Harvard University, Roderick MacFarquhar offered helpful suggestions on the manuscript and provided guidance and assistance throughout the process of revision and publication. Jacques de Lisle provided insightful criticisms and served as a constant source of advice on various aspects of the book's publication. Yuen Foong Khong and Ezra Vogel gave generously of their time to read the manuscript and offer valuable suggestions. Nancy Hearst provided much useful bibliographical advice and was a constant source of good humor. My wife, Page, patiently provided encouragement, advice and expert assistance. She has helped make this project truly enjoyable.

The generous assistance of these people has improved the book and taught me a great deal. The errors that remain are mine alone.

Kevin P. Lane

Note on Romanization

Since this book covers a long historical period and includes names and terms from both Cantonese and Mandarin, romanization is somewhat problematic. In order to minimize confusion, no attempt is made to standardize all words according to a single system. Rather, the book simply uses the most common romanizations of names and terms from Cantonese and Mandarin. Most references to the Nationalist period use Wade-Giles, and those from the CCP period use *pinyin*. For those words that are known in more than one system, *pinyin* is favored. Likewise, most place names are romanized using the *pinyin* system, except those that are commonly known otherwise (such as locations in Hong Kong). "Canton" is used throughout the book to refer to the city also known as Guangzhou, and "Guangdong" refers to the province adjacent to Hong Kong. "Beijing" is used consistently in favor of "Peking" or "Peiping."

K.P.L.

1

The Hong Kong Question

Since Prime Minister Margaret Thatcher's historic visit to Beijing in September 1982, considerable attention has been focused on the question of Hong Kong's future. The planned return of Hong Kong to the People's Republic of China in 1997, after 155 years as a British colony, has inspired widespread speculation about the future of its lifestyle and economy. The issue has dominated media coverage in Hong Kong and has received increasing attention in the West. Scholarly research on Hong Kong also has grown dramatically since the early 1980s. The nature of Hong Kong's relationship with the mainland, the process of negotiating the Sino-British agreement on Hong Kong's future, the drafting of Hong Kong's post–1997 Basic Law, and the territory's internal political developments are among the issues that have become popular subjects for research and analysis.

Such widespread concern with the "1997 question" or "Hong Kong question," as the issue has come to be known, is understandable. The return of ceded and leased territory to its original owner, while not unprecedented, is highly unusual in the history of decolonization. The issue is made more complex by Hong Kong's status as one of the world's largest international financial centers, a bastion of laissez-faire capitalism that has experienced one of the world's most impressive rates of economic growth over the past three decades, and the home of a large number of refugees from the Chinese mainland. The prospect of integrating the colony into the underdeveloped, socialist PRC has created unique challenges for the British and Chinese governments. The outcome of their work will have important implications for Sino-British relations and for Hong Kong's role in the international economy.

The Hong Kong question has attracted further attention because of the unique nature of the arrangements made for the territory's status as a part of the PRC. According to the concept of "one country, two systems," which the Chinese leadership has hailed as "the cornerstone for the peaceful realization of the reunification of our motherland,"[1]

Hong Kong will become a Special Administrative Region (SAR) of the PRC. In order to guarantee continued "stability and prosperity" in the SAR, the Chinese central government has promised that Hong Kong will maintain its existing social and economic systems for at least fifty years, will select its leaders from among local residents and will enjoy a high degree of autonomy in its internal affairs. These promises may be difficult to keep, however. The establishment of an SAR under the "one country, two systems" formula is a radically new concept that will be difficult to implement precisely as planned. Yet most observers agree that only careful implementation of the agreement on Hong Kong's future will allow the territory to remain stable and prosperous after 1997.

Academic and political considerations aside, the Hong Kong question has become an important subject of debate and research because of the profound effect it will have on the colony's 5.6 million residents, whose futures hang in the balance. Many of those residents are refugees from the mainland who ponder with understandable anxiety the prospect of living again under Communist rule. Many others were born and raised in Hong Kong; they form a newly emerged generation of Hong Kong "belongers" who think of Hong Kong as their only home and feel a genuine commitment to the colony. For these and other Hong Kong residents, the future of the way of life they have come to value appears uncomfortably uncertain.

Much of the discussion surrounding the Hong Kong question has consisted of speculation about what will happen to the colony's society, economy and politics after it becomes an SAR. This overwhelming focus on the future reflects a legitimate concern for the livelihood of the territory and its residents, as well as a certain fascination with the unusual circumstances in which Hong Kong now finds itself. In the course of this discussion, however, little attention has been paid to the past. Few scholars have examined in depth the nature of Chinese policy toward Hong Kong before the 1997 issue gained prominence.

This book takes a step in that direction by analyzing Chinese rhetoric and actions concerning Hong Kong since the establishment of the Chinese Republic in 1912. It traces consistencies and variations in stated policy toward Hong Kong and compares principle with practice by examining actions that Chinese governments have taken toward the colony.[2] This historical approach serves two major purposes. First, by providing a long-term perspective on Chinese policy toward Hong Kong that includes the actions of different regimes operating under widely varying domestic and international circumstances, it helps clarify the issues that are crucial to understanding current Chinese policy. A historical analysis cannot predict future behavior, but it at least may illuminate those factors that will continue to play a role in policy decisions.

Second, a historical study of China's Hong Kong policy is instructive for other areas of Chinese policy. The Hong Kong case is unique in many respects. Nevertheless, Chinese leaders' efforts to reconcile anti-imperialist principles with the practical dilemmas presented by British administration in Hong Kong may indicate how they seek to resolve other foreign policy problems that bring principle and practice into direct conflict. Hong Kong also occupies a critical juncture in two of the PRC's top domestic policy goals: economic modernization and national reunification. As a result, Hong Kong's status and its special relationship with the mainland will continue to be a major concern for Chinese policy makers well into the future.

Origins of the Problem

PRC officials typically refer to Hong Kong as "a question left over from history." This formula has allowed them to avoid facing the issue directly; as a problem left by the Qing dynasty, it can be treated differently from other foreign policy issues. But the statement is also true. Hong Kong was acquired in the nineteenth century by a powerful, colonialist Great Britain from a militarily weak, imperial Chinese government, under conditions radically different from those that exist today.

The means by which Great Britain obtained the land that became the colony of Hong Kong have been discussed elsewhere.[3] It is important to recall, however, that the colony consists of three parcels of land. Hong Kong Island, 29.2 square miles of what was at the time mostly rock, was ceded by the Chinese "in perpetuity" at the end of the First Opium War, by the 1842 Treaty of Nanjing. While not regarded by the British Foreign Office at the time as a valuable piece of territory, Hong Kong Island at least gave the British their own trading base near Canton to replace Portuguese Macau and positioned them in the center of one of the world's finest natural harbors. After the Second Opium War of 1858–1860, when British and French forces sacked Beijing and destroyed the Summer Palace, Britain demanded that China cede the tip of the Kowloon Peninsula and Stonecutters Island, strategically located at the entrance to the harbor. Totalling only 4.1 square miles, this parcel of land ceded by the 1860 Convention of Beijing afforded the British better protection of their position on Hong Kong Island and gave them a foothold on the Chinese mainland.

Following the Chinese defeat in the Sino-Japanese War of 1894–1895, Germany pressured the weakened Manchu government to provide it with a port in China, finally succeeding in 1898, when it acquired a ninety-nine–year lease on Jiaozhou Bay in eastern Shandong Province. Russia immediately followed suit, gaining a twenty-five–year lease on

Port Arthur (Jinzhou Bay) and Dalian Bay (later called Dairen by the Japanese) on the Liaodong Peninsula. To counter these acquisitions, Great Britain demanded and secured a leasehold at the port of Weihaiwei in eastern Shandong. The lease was to remain in effect for as long as Russia retained Port Arthur.

In South China, France joined the grab for territory by securing a ninety-nine–year lease on Guangzhou Bay in southern Guangdong province. The British, who for several years had been contemplating the expansion of Hong Kong for commercial and defense reasons, took advantage of the French move to demand a similar arrangement on the Kowloon Peninsula. Under the 1898 Convention of Beijing, China leased to Great Britain for ninety-nine years an area that was to be called the New Territories, covering 370.4 square miles, including 235 islands and two bays.[4]

It is the imminent expiration of the New Territories lease that has created the crisis over Hong Kong's future. Of course, the lease covers only a portion (albeit a large one) of the territory currently administered by Great Britain, but the British and Chinese agree that the colony must be dealt with as a single entity. In practical terms, the New Territories provides much of the colony's manufacturing, water and power. Cut off from the New Territories, the rest of the colony could not survive. For administrative purposes, the British themselves have since 1898 considered all three territories as a single unit. And from the PRC's perspective, each of the three treaties involving Hong Kong is invalid in international law, so distinctions among their terms are technically meaningless.

Since the 1920s, both the Kuomintang (KMT or Nationalist Party) and the Chinese Communist Party (CCP) have included Hong Kong's treaties in a group of agreements signed by the Qing's Manchu government that are considered "unequal." Their argument, that treaties imposed on the Qing government under threat of military force cannot be considered valid, is persuasive. The treaties of 1842 and 1860 were classic examples of British "gunboat diplomacy," and the 1898 Convention of Beijing was signed with a weak, divided China that had been badly defeated in a war with Japan. When Hong Kong and Kowloon were granted to Great Britain, no equivalent term for "cession" had previously existed in the Chinese language, and only in 1864 was a Western text on international law translated into Chinese.[5] The notion of inequality in treaties has been recognized by both the 1969 Vienna Convention on the Law of Treaties and the International Court of Justice. And while an acknowledgement of inequality does not necessarily make a treaty invalid,[6] both the Nationalists and the Communists have argued at different times that the treaties concerning Hong Kong are not valid in international law.

The Hong Kong Question

Great Britain's lease on the New Territories, which comprises about ninety-four percent of the colony's territory, expires at midnight on June 30, 1997. On July 1, the Union Jack will be lowered and the Queen-appointed colonial governor will leave, after which the Crown Colony of Hong Kong will begin its new status as a Special Administrative Region of the PRC. Anticipation of the event has become intense. References to 1997 increasingly dominated Hong Kong society in the 1980s: in the media, in schools, in business, in public debate and, not least, in the minds of Hong Kong's residents, who must decide whether to stay or pursue a life abroad.

But the attention focused on 1997 has overshadowed the fact that the question of Hong Kong's status is not at all a new issue for mainland policy makers. Beginning in the late 1910s, China's claim to sovereignty over the colony, supported by persuasive legal and moral arguments, has been made with increasing passion. That claim was convincing enough that as early as the 1920s, the British Foreign Office discussed the issue of its return. In the late 1920s and 1930s, most other foreign-held territories, concessions, spheres of interest and extraterritorial rights in China were forfeited, and the United States backed Chinese requests to recover Hong Kong, but the colony remained in British hands. In the 1940s, Hong Kong seemed to come perilously close to being returned to the mainland, but it emerged from World War II and Japanese occupation intact, with a new British-appointed government. After the Communists came to power in 1949, they left no doubt about their intention to recover Hong Kong, but their claims brought only mild disruptions to the colony's rapidly-developing economy. By the late 1980s, few people questioned the justice of the Chinese claim to sovereignty over Hong Kong, a territory that was taken by force from China and whose population is ninety-eight percent ethnic Chinese, though many doubted the wisdom of returning the colony to the PRC.

Despite China's repeated assertion of its claim to Hong Kong, the colony has grown and prospered under British rule. Originally "a barren rock with hardly a house upon it," as Foreign Secretary Lord Palmerston described Hong Kong Island when the British occupied it in 1841, Hong Kong by the end of the nineteenth century became the hub of South China's trade. As the Chinese nationalist movement grew dramatically following the May Fourth Incident of 1919 and foreign-held rights and territories were successively forfeited, Hong Kong prospered as a successful entrepôt port. Following the Communist victory, the colony became a haven for Shanghai's refugee industrialists, who under the added pressure of a United Nations trade embargo against the PRC, helped turn the colony into a manufacturing center. During the 1960s and 1970s, Hong Kong experienced impressive economic growth, eventually developing into one of the world's major centers of trade and finance.

Hong Kong's growth and prosperity as a British colony alongside a strongly anti-imperialist China, and eventually in a postwar world that rapidly decolonized, appears paradoxical. Yet it is this paradox, between China's territorial claims over Hong Kong on the one hand, and its willingness to permit Hong Kong's continued existence as a British colony on the other, that reveals the fundamental elements of Chinese policy toward Hong Kong throughout much of this century.

At the heart of the Hong Kong question is the issue of sovereignty. The re-exercise of sovereignty over Hong Kong has long been an inviolable principle for Chinese leaders. Though before the 1980s they never explained in detail what the term meant in reference to Hong Kong, it was apparent that sovereignty included the absolute right to exercise legislative and jurisdictional powers over the territory and its people. The Communists adopted a particularly strict view of sovereignty that was influenced by Soviet theories of international law, but in general the CCP and the KMT understood the exercise of sovereignty over Hong Kong to mean the same thing: the departure of British administration and the political, legal and administrative reunification of Hong Kong with the mainland.[7]

But while the principle of sovereignty has been considered an unassailable element of China's Hong Kong policy, its realization for both the Nationalists and Communists has been fraught with complications. For years, China's military and economic weakness kept it from pushing territorial claims over Hong Kong. The British were unwilling to return the colony (while the idea was raised on several occasions, the dominant opinions in the British government consistently opposed it) and the Chinese, especially prior to 1949, were in no position to take it back by force. In international forums, the Chinese government failed to carry the political weight necessary to force a resolution of the issue. Furthermore, throughout the first half of this century the Chinese were preoccupied with matters of more immediate concern than Hong Kong's status. When the Nationalists began extensive renegotiation of the Qing dynasty's "unequal treaties" with the foreign powers, Hong Kong was less prominent than the treaty ports and foreign concessions in the Northeast, where the real bite of the foreign presence, including widespread mining, railroad and extraterritorial rights, was felt. And though for several years during the 1920s the British were singled out as China's main target of antiforeign agitation, for most of the first half of the twentieth century China's main enemy was Japan, not Great Britain.

The quest for sovereignty over Hong Kong in this century has been further complicated by the desire of successive Chinese governments to earn respect for China as a responsible actor in international affairs. This was a major goal of the KMT from the birth of the Republic in 1912 and became a central element of the Nationalist regime's foreign policy after 1928. In light of the extent to which the KMT sought foreign assistance in resolving China's economic and political difficulties, government officials felt pressured to prove that China was a responsible, friendly power. These concerns created disincentives to pushing claims, however just they were believed to be, that might be seen as hostile to the British and other foreign powers. Communist leaders felt similar pressures. After 1949, despite strident anti-imperialist rhetoric and a strong anticapitalist posture, top PRC policy makers, including Chairman Mao Zedong and Premier Zhou Enlai, were reluctant to take actions toward Hong Kong that could be viewed as irresponsible and damage the PRC's international reputation.

The benefits that British Hong Kong has provided the mainland also have proven to be strong incentives against pressing the claim to sovereignty. Since its inception as a British colony, Hong Kong has served as a door to the world for China, a convenient location to gain access to the ideas and technologies of the West. It has provided safe haven, too, for individuals and groups who at different times have been out of favor in the mainland, and has served as a useful, well-protected staging ground for political activities, including propaganda, communications, espionage and fund-raising. Throughout this century, Hong Kong has also provided important economic benefits to the mainland through bilateral trade, loans, unrequited gifts and investment capital.

The Hong Kong question, then, is to the Chinese not merely about the expiration of the New Territories lease. Rather, it concerns the solution of a difficult problem of domestic and foreign policy: how to resolve the inherent tension between a claim to sovereignty over territory that is legitimately considered to be Chinese, and the strong incentives that exist against pressing that claim.

China's Hong Kong Policy

Seen from this perspective, the Hong Kong question has existed since the issue of the colony's return was first raised in the 1910s. Since then, successive Chinese governments have attempted to resolve the issue. While there have been differences in their approaches, the basic elements have remained consistent. On the principle of sovereignty, the Chinese have been unyielding. Official statements have argued that Hong Kong was, is, and always will be Chinese territory; its return to the mainland is viewed as not only legally and morally right but inevitable in the course of history. At the same time, actual Chinese policies toward Hong Kong have accepted, even supported, its status quo as a British colony. With a few notable exceptions, Chinese policy makers have carefully avoided taking actions that might threaten British rule in the colony, while they have built an amiable relationship with strong economic ties from which both the Chinese mainland and Hong Kong have prospered.

Chinese officials frequently have justified their accommodation of a British colony on Chinese soil by pointing to nineteenth century events that were beyond their control. In accordance with their anti-imperialist principles, both the Nationalists and Communists at different times have promised to recover Hong Kong, but only at a suitable moment—"when conditions are ripe," as the PRC's well-known statement of the problem put it. The advantage of this formulation has been that it sacrifices neither the principle of Chinese sovereignty nor the practical advantages of maintaining Hong Kong's colonial status quo. When the time arrived that sovereignty could be exercised without sacrificing those benefits, negotiations would be undertaken to return Hong Kong to the mainland. While the KMT in the 1940s expected that opportunity to come soon, after 1949 the CCP clearly preferred not to resolve the Hong Kong question for a very long time.

Time has run out for Hong Kong, however. Beginning in the late 1970s, investors nervous about loans and leases whose terms would extend beyond June 30, 1997, expressed their anxieties to the British leadership in Hong Kong. Their concerns led Governor Sir Murray MacLehose to raise the issue with Chinese leader Deng Xiaoping in 1979. While Deng was reportedly unconcerned about the impending deadline, telling MacLehose that Hong Kong investors should "set their hearts at ease," the Chinese and British governments began to study in detail how the issue of Hong Kong's status could be resolved. After Prime Minister Margaret Thatcher's visit to Beijing in September 1982, negotiations over arrangements for the colony's future were begun. Two years later, the two sides signed an agreement to return Hong Kong to full Chinese sovereignty on July 1, 1997, as the PRC's first Special Administrative Region. By the end of the decade, the complex process of transition from colony to SAR was well under way.

The Sino-British negotiations over Hong Kong's future and the process of drafting the Basic Law that will serve as the SAR's "constitution" have forced the Chinese for the first time to resolve the contradictions that have long been at the heart of their Hong Kong policy. They have done so in a manner characteristic of Chinese policy since the 1920s. The fundamental principle of Chinese sovereignty, including sole legislative and jurisdictional rights exclusive of any third party involvement, remains inviolable. Within that context, however, the Chinese are willing to allow the SAR to retain substantial autonomy for at least fifty years. In other words, the Chinese are seeking to retain both sovereignty and the so-called "status quo." This will be much more difficult in practice than in theory, however. Already the PRC has discovered that simply maintaining its *claim* to sovereignty while allowing Hong Kong to continue as a British colony is far less complicated than recovering sovereignty and shouldering the responsibility for administration it entails. The years leading up to 1997, which will include substantive reform of the colony's political structure, will provide telling indications of how likely the Chinese are to succeed.

With considerable fanfare, the PRC leadership has adopted "one country, two systems" and "Hong Kong people ruling Hong Kong" as an ideal solution to the problem of Hong Kong's future. This book does not attempt to suggest whether that solution will succeed after 1997. It argues that, in the long history of the Hong Kong question, Chinese policy makers have pursued similar goals and have responded in similar ways to incentives presented by Hong Kong's unusual status. Throughout this century, they have successfully maintained both China's claim to sovereignty over Hong Kong and the benefits the colony provides to the mainland. After 1997, the dual goals of realizing that claim to sovereignty and maintaining Hong Kong's way of life will prove to be an even greater challenge.

Notes

1. Speech by Xu Jiatun, director of New China News Agency Hong Kong Branch, published in *Hsin Wan Pao*, April 4, 1985, in Foreign Broadcast Information Service, *Daily Report: China*, April 4, 1985, W5.

2. The term "policy" in this book refers both to broad goals and to the specific measures taken to achieve them. In places where the distinction may not be obvious, efforts have been made to clarify the usage.

3. See G. B. Endacott, *A History of Hong Kong*, 2nd ed. (Hong Kong: Oxford University Press, 1977). On the lease of the New Territories, see Peter Wesley-Smith, *Unequal Treaty, 1898–1997: China, Great Britain and Hong Kong's New Territories* (Hong Kong: Oxford University Press, 1983).

4. For details on British reasons for seeking to acquire the New Territories and on the Sino-British negotiations that led to the lease, see Wesley-Smith, *Unequal Treaty*, 11–44.

5. Anthony Dicks, "Treaty, Grant, Usage or Sufferance? Legal Aspects of the Status of Hong Kong," *China Quarterly*, 95 (Sept. 1983):443–44.

6. See discussion in Wesley-Smith, *Unequal Treaty*, 184–87.

7. For a discussion of the PRC's views on sovereignty as they relate to the Hong Kong question, see Dicks, "Treaty," 427–55.

2

Emerging Chinese Nationalism and Hong Kong, 1912–1927

The frail Republican government that emerged to replace the fallen Qing dynasty on January 1, 1912, faced major challenges, not the least of which was the continued foreign presence in China. One of the Qing dynasty's legacies had been the acquisition by foreign governments of "extraterritorial" rights, which allowed foreigners in China exemption from local jurisdiction. In addition, Japan and many Western countries, including Great Britain, Russia, France, Germany, the United States and others, had acquired a variety of other special rights and privileges on Chinese territory. Foreign countries retained colonies in the Northeast and Southeast and controlled mining and railroad rights. Foreign settlements, in which Chinese jurisdiction did not apply, existed in several major cities. China's external trade was operated through "treaty ports," in which foreigners controlled the customs service, depriving the central government of an important source of revenue. In the Canton delta, British interests dominated shipping, trade and finance. From the middle of the nineteenth century through the first half of the twentieth century, this entrenched foreign presence remained a central element of the Chinese political landscape. It also became a ripe target for protest.

Following the 1911 Revolution, political discourse in China focused increasingly on foreign encroachment and its resultant compromise of Chinese sovereignty. Beginning in the late 1910s, China's political and intellectual elite made their first petitions for the return of China's territories—including the British Crown Colony of Hong Kong—and over the course of the 1920s those pleas grew in number and popular support. Partly in response to growing antiforeign sentiment and partly in an attempt to remove restrictions on their own freedom of maneuver, Chinese officials for the first time began to make determined efforts to abrogate the unequal treaties.

The Qing's Legacy of Foreign Encroachment

Chinese leaders since 1912 have commonly blamed the Qing dynasty's Manchu government for the regime of foreign control created by the unequal treaties. The treaties and the national humiliation associated with them, Chiang Kai-shek wrote, "must ultimately be attributed to political corruption and especially to the decline of the arts and sciences and of social life during the Manchu Dynasty."[1] Most scholarship on the Qing dynasty is somewhat more generous than Chiang, however, arguing that the Manchus had little choice but to accede to the carving up of their territory. Considering the overwhelming military advantage enjoyed by the foreign powers, the Manchu government was ill-suited to force them out and carried little leverage into treaty negotiations. It is for just this reason that the Chinese were later to call the treaties "unequal."

While an organized nationalist movement was not to emerge in China until the 1920s, popular opposition to foreign presence was apparent well before the fall of the Qing. Resentment became particularly strong in the years following the Japanese victory in the 1894–1895 Sino-Japanese War. The 1895 Treaty of Shimonoseki, which ended the war, granted major territorial concessions to the Japanese and brought national disgrace to the Chinese, who had long considered Japan something of a cultural "younger brother." It also ushered in a frantic grab for territory and special rights by the other powers, in what became known as the "scramble for concessions." In the few years that followed, much of Northeast China and parts of East and Southeast China were brought under foreign control.

Growing domestic opposition to these developments erupted at the turn of the century in the form of the Boxer Uprising. The Boxers were an organized force comprised mostly of poor peasants whose claims of invincibility relied on magic spells, trances and sacred boxing. Originally a revolutionary movement, in late 1899 the Boxers joined forces with conservative Manchu officials and adopted the slogan, "Uphold the Qing! Exterminate the foreigner!" After holding foreigners under seige in Beijing for two months in the summer of 1900, the Boxers fell to an international rescue force. The only attempt by the Qing rulers to fight foreign encroachment aggressively thus ended in failure and further humiliation, as the Boxer Protocol of September 1901 punished Qing officials, called for the destruction of Qing forts and imposed a huge indemnity on the Manchu government.

The Boxer Uprising was limited to North China, contained by independent-minded provincial governors unwilling to challenge the foreign powers directly. Hong Kong experienced only an increase in the normal flow of refugees to the colony. At about the same time the Boxers were becoming active in the North, however, Chinese in Guangdong mounted their own opposition to British colonization.

When the 375-square-mile expanse of land known as the Kowloon Leased Territory, or the New Territories, was leased to the British under the 1898 Convention of Beijing, it was inhabited by about 100,000 people. The British lease on the territory took effect on July 1, 1898, and they began preparations for occupying the territory in the fall of that year. New Territories residents also began their own preparations, however. When British troops moved to occupy the territory in the spring of 1899, they were met with an armed, organized resistance force. The men had apparently been recruited and trained for weeks prior to the occupation, by local leaders reluctant to give up their land and power. After several skirmishes with the British, the resistance forces made their strongest stand at Tai Po, near the current site of The Chinese University of Hong Kong, where more than two thousand Chinese men armed with heavy weapons clashed repeatedly with British troops. Despite their valiant efforts, the Chinese were no match for superior British forces. They suffered heavy losses and were defeated easily.[2]

The determined opposition of Chinese peasants in the New Territories surprised the British, who expected a smoother transfer of authority. And it was clearly a local phenomenon, not directed from Beijing. But both the local resistance and its failure are representative of the nationwide difficulties the Manchu government faced in dealing with foreign powers during the nineteenth and early twentieth centuries. Despite increasing resentment of foreign encroachment, China's leaders lacked the national authority and the military power to oppose the foreign presence. By the time the Qing dynasty collapsed in late 1911, Japan and the Western Powers had forced open 35 ports, obtained 27 concessions and constructed international settlements in 27 cities. China's reparations bill before the Boxer Protocol was already three times the income of the imperial government.[3] In its last decade, the Qing government in Beijing seemed to be biding time. It would take a new government and fundamentally different circumstances to end the scourge of foreign domination and to begin the long process of returning Chinese territory, including Hong Kong, to Chinese sovereignty.

The Early Chinese Republic

On October 10, 1911, an uprising in the city of Wuchang, in central China, sparked a series of rebellions throughout the country that finally forced the collapse of the Qing dynasty. The timing of this defeat was a surprise to revolutionary leaders; Sun Yat-sen, leader of the revolutionary movement, was on a fund-raising trip in the United States and learned of the events while in Denver. The new leaders had been fighting for more than a decade to overthrow the Manchu rulers, but they were unprepared for governing and had mapped out only vague programs. Furthermore, the new Chinese Republic inherited the substantial burdens of its predecessor. The Manchu government had left an impoverished, politically fractured nation. And while the issue of foreign presence in China was by no means the only one on their agenda, the new leaders had inherited the commitments and humiliations of the old treaties, as well as a mandate to do something about them. The Manchus had been a target for criticism regarding foreign imperialism in China, and many Chinese elites now looked to the new Republican government to deal quickly and decisively with that problem.

Quick results would be difficult to achieve, however. One problem was that, for all its promise, the "revolution" in China had brought little substantive change. National unification remained an elusive goal in the face of regional divisions and the absence of a strong central government with economic and military power. Despite Great Britain's symbolic statement in the 1902 MacKay Treaty with China that it would relinquish all extraterritorial rights when "conditions warrant" (the Japanese, American and Swedish governments made similar noncommittal declarations in 1912), foreign governments had not demonstrated a willingness to withdraw from China on their own initiative.

This predicament was reflected in Sun Yat-sen's decision to abdicate the presidency in favor of the powerful Qing general, Yuan Shih-k'ai, who took the oath of office in March 1912. Hardly a committed Republican, Yuan at least held out the promise of uniting China's provincial military leaders and of using his considerable political experience to deal successfully with the foreigners. But Yuan's record was one of skillful accommodation rather than opposition to foreign presence—he had opposed the Boxers, for example—and he neither possessed the military forces necessary to eradicate the foreign presence nor was inclined to do so. Yuan's policy declaration of October 10, 1913, was typically conservative:

> I hereby declare that all treaties, conventions and international agreements entered into between the former Manchu and Provisional Republican Governments of the one part and the foreign governments of the other part shall be strictly observed, and that all contracts duly concluded by the former governments with foreign companies and individuals shall also be strictly observed, and, further, that all rights, privileges and immunities enjoyed by foreigners in China by virtue of international engagements, national enactments and established usages are hereby confirmed. This

declaration I make with a view to the maintenance of international amity and peace.[4]

Yuan did as he promised. Between 1912 and his death in June 1916, the Chinese government made no attempt to seek abrogation of treaties with the Powers. Rather, it concluded a series of new treaties, most involving railroad rights and loan agreements. China's burgeoning nationalism had not yet developed the force necessary to pose a serious threat to widespread foreign interests in the country. In addition, Yuan's strong-arm measures to weaken the newly formed KMT, to dismantle the Republican government and to concentrate power in his own hands effectively removed potential sources of antiforeign organization.

Yuan was not alone in favoring a cautious approach on treaty issues, however. The Manifesto on the Organization of the KMT, dated August 1912, emphasized domestic construction over antiforeignism and urged respect for the status quo and principles of diplomacy in international affairs. The party's platform, issued a year later, admitted that China had been compelled to make "concessions" to foreign countries, but recommended an accommodative approach to the problem: "In the present circumstances, China is not yet in a position to cope with the foreign powers effectively. So it is desirable to have them maintain their established policies without upsetting the status quo."[5]

The 1911 Revolution and Hong Kong

The new government's accommodative attitude toward foreign interests in China was also reflected in relations between the mainland and Hong Kong. The colony's status was never in doubt. The dominant issue in China–Hong Kong relations between late 1910 and early 1912 was the negotiation of an agreement for through traffic on the Kowloon-Canton Railway. Negotiators met throughout 1911 and reached an agreement in the fall. In a christening ceremony on October 10 that celebrated Sino-British friendship, Chao Ch'ing-hua, managing director of the Chinese segment, noted the "unwavering interests of the two governments both in this railway and in the friendship of the two nations."[6]

Less than four weeks later, on November 6, news that Beijing had fallen (which later turned out to be erroneous) reached Hong Kong. Chinese in Hong Kong reportedly "went mad" rejoicing, celebrating in the streets with flags and firecrackers. Hong Kong Governor Sir Frederick Lugard called it "the most amazing outburst which has ever been seen and heard in the history of this colony." The public celebration lasted, with the explicit permission of the Hong Kong government, for two days.[7] Five days later, Guangdong province declared in favor of the

Republican Party, further arousing nationalist sentiment in the colony. According to Lugard, "The Chinese of Hong Kong almost to a man not only sympathize with the Revolution but are profoundly moved by it."[8] He also noted an increase in "rowdiness" in the form of attacks on police and insults to Europeans after the establishment of the new government in Guangdong.[9] Though inspired by events across the border, this antiforeign activity was unorganized, and its scope and duration were limited.

The Republican revolutionaries occupied positions on the Hong Kong border and at frontier train stations without incident. They clearly were under orders to respect the boundary; on only one reported occasion did a group of several revolutionaries cross the border into Hong Kong's New Territories, where they were arrested by Hong Kong border guards. Upon questioning it became apparent that the soldiers had lost their way and crossed the border by mistake. Their guns were returned and they were released.[10]

The general attitude in Canton, as among wealthy Chinese in Hong Kong, was that conditions should be stabilized as soon as possible. As early as February 1911, the viceroy of Guangdong had approached Governor Lugard to request advice on how to establish and run a constitutional government.[11] Once established, the new government was anxious to remain on good terms with the colony. Lugard noted on November 21, 1911, that the revolutionary government appeared ready to indemnify Hong Kong on the recently-signed railway agreement.[12] The new officials in Canton respected Hong Kong residents' expertise and valued the intimate ties between the two economies. They watched Hong Kong closely and readily solicited advice from its prominent Chinese residents. "The leading men here are looked to and consulted by the Revolutionary leaders at every step," wrote Lugard.[13] As for dealing with the increase in "rowdiness," a top Cantonese official wrote a letter to the Chinese Press Association in Hong Kong deprecating rowdyism and strikes and urging members to use their influence to assist the Hong Kong government in maintaining order. He also promised to prevent an influx of "bad characters" into the colony.[14] And Sun Yat-sen, according to a British official he met with in China, emphasized that he was "especially anxious to work in full harmony with the British Government in matters concerning China."[15]

In the months that followed, the new government at Canton continued to look favorably upon Hong Kong. Trade, a matter of crucial importance for both sides, resumed quickly, as did through train service. Hong Kong's Chinese residents also became targets for scores of fund-raising projects. Guangdong's economy desperately needed financial assistance, and Chinese entrepreneurs in the colony were obvious targets for patriotic pleas of support, as they had been before and have been since. Hong Kong Chinese were skeptical of many of the schemes in which they were invited to participate, and they often were distrustful of the men who backed them, but to refuse to subscribe would be viewed as unpatriotic, a label few Chinese in Hong Kong or elsewhere were willing to wear. Revolutionary government officials and newly formed financial companies appealed to Hong Kong residents' "burning patriotism" and their desire to save China from "eternal disgrace."[16] Their efforts apparently paid off. The British consul general at Canton reported not long after the revolution that, "The new government is being well supported by subscription."[17] Indeed, one million dollars was reported subscribed by Hong Kong merchants to the Canton government in November 1911, with an additional two to three million dollars supplied within less than a year after that.[18]

While the Hong Kong government did not object to local Chinese providing financial assistance, the political relationship between Hong Kong's Chinese residents and the mainland government was a more delicate issue. It became a matter of dispute in late 1912, when authorities in Canton announced that Chinese residents in Hong Kong would be allowed to elect delegates to represent them in the Chinese Senate.[19] The Hong Kong government, always suspicious of potential attempts to undermine its authority, particularly in light of the close ties between Hong Kong Chinese and their mainland compatriots, objected to the idea. Nevertheless, a meeting of Hong Kong "District Societies" was held in January 1913 to elect members to travel to Beijing and participate in the election of a Chinese resident of Hong Kong to the Chinese National Assembly.[20] In the end, however, the Hong Kong government was able to pressure local residents to abandon their plans. Elections were held on February 19 in Beijing, with no Hong Kong delegates present.[21]

The official Chinese response to British intervention in this issue was reserved. In a note to the British ambassador in Beijing in May 1913, the Chinese Foreign Ministry said it "entertained strong objections" to the British refusal to allow Hong Kong representatives to the National Assembly. But the note reassured the British government that no challenge was being made to colonial authority in Hong Kong. The proposed delegates from Hong Kong, it was explained, were to participate in the "Electoral College of Chinese Resident Abroad," which included delegates from, among other places, New South Wales.[22] The Foreign Ministry document explained that the election did not infringe on Great Britain's "sovereign rights" and did not "injure Great Britain's right of governing her dependencies."[23] Nor did the Republican government attempt to force the issue against British wishes. In later years, Hong Kong residents would be permitted to serve as delegates to political bodies in China. Still, the mainland government's claim to the allegiance of Chinese residents in Hong Kong remained an underlying element of Chinese policy and on occasion became a source of friction between the Hong Kong and Chinese governments.

The Twenty-One Demands

The first few years of the Chinese Republic, then, were fairly smooth ones for the Powers and their territories, including the British in Hong Kong. If the Chinese were awakening to a new nationalism, it had not yet been harnessed or focused against specific policies, territories or countries. To the British in Hong Kong, little was substantively different from life under the Manchu government.

The "Twenty-One Demands" began to change all that, however. On January 18, 1915, Japan handed to China a list of demands designed to put southern Manchuria, eastern Inner Mongolia and Shandong Province under Japanese jurisdiction. Under a further Japanese ultimatum on May 7, Yuan Shih-k'ai's government conceded to most of the demands, setting aside one group, which would have given Japan indirect control of the Chinese central government, for future discussion.

After signing the agreement, however, the government issued a statement asserting that it had been "constrained to comply fully with the terms of the ultimatum."[24] This is the first public reference to an argument that was to become a central part of the Chinese position on Hong Kong and other treaty issues, that the conditions under which an agreement was reached could affect its legitimacy.

Five days later, the Republican government issued a Presidential Mandate that reflected growing frustration over continued infringement of China's sovereignty. As a result of the cession and lease of strategic coastal areas during the Qing dynasty, the Mandate charged, "the means of defence were practically lost to China, whose people have since not been able to enjoy peace." In accordance with the legislature's request, Yuan ordered that, "Hereafter, no port, bay or island along the coast of China will be ceded or leased to any foreign country. The Ministries of War and Marine and the officials on the seacoast are hereby made responsible for the defence of the same so that the sovereignty of the nation may be consolidated."[25] Despite its symbolic significance, the declaration in reality was superfluous, since by 1915 virtually all coastal regions that could be considered strategically valuable were already controlled by foreign governments. And the Chinese government, at least at this point, was not in a position to attempt to recoup its "means of defence."

Japan's Twenty-One Demands incited an angry popular response that went well beyond the government's position. A boycott of Japanese goods was organized almost immediately and lasted for several months before President Yuan ordered it halted. Other anti-Japanese boycotts, strikes and mass rallies began to occur with frequency. Well-known writers increasingly published their protests in the popular press, as a previously amorphous antiforeignism finally found an identifiable target and set of goals.

In Hong Kong, at least at first, there was no reason to fear that this popular nationalist sentiment would threaten the British position. On the contrary, with Japan apparently poised and determined to swallow the whole of China, the British presence in Hong Kong appeared to offer a potential deterrent to further Japanese aggression. Hong Kong's secretary for Chinese affairs reported in the spring of 1915 that the official Chinese disposition regarding the British was "excellent." "The way they see it," he explained, is that "under any circumstances Japan's power cannot be broken for a long time . . . so it will be better if Great Britain can still be there to watch Japan."[26]

But the effects of the Twenty-One Demands were to reverberate later. This Japanese threat was one in a series of events that would increasingly incite the Chinese to challenge foreign presence on Chinese soil and would have an important impact on the development of China's domestic politics. What at first appeared to be a struggle against the major enemy, Japan, was soon to become a struggle to throw off all the "shackles" of foreign domination, including those on Hong Kong.

Diplomatic Efforts
at Regaining Territorial Sovereignty

The question of revising or abrogating treaties signed by the Manchus came under serious discussion at least as early as the mid–1910s and was profoundly influenced by the humiliation of the Twenty-One Demands. China's position on sovereignty over leased territories, which remains a central and sensitive issue in its Hong Kong policy today, was expressed in a 1916 article by Wunsz (also Wen-Sze) King, a Chinese diplomat who was to play an important role in diplomatic efforts concerning treaty relations. King argued that "reservation of sovereignty" by the lessor country, which had been included explicitly in lease agreements with Germany, France and Russia and implicitly in British leases (for example, by permitting Chinese naval vessels to travel unhindered in the New Territories' Mirs Bay and Deep Bay) was unquestionable.[27]

M. T. Z. Tyau, a lecturer at Qinghua University in Beijing, argued in a Chinese academic journal in 1917 that treaties should be revised so as to end extraterritorial rights in China. Furthermore, all leased territories, including Hong Kong's New Territories, should be returned to China, "since the circumstances which had called them into existence had fundamentally altered." Tyau argued that the treaties had been imposed by a superior force on a weaker one, foreshadowing later appeals that would use the term "unequal treaties," and pointed out that China's new political circumstances since the fall of the Qing dynasty made the doctrine of *rebus sic stantibus*, or "so long as conditions remain the same," applicable.[28] According to this doctrine, which has a long and controversial history in international law, the terms of a treaty may be deemed invalid if the circumstances under which it was negotiated become fundamentally altered.[29]

In a later article, Tyau was optimistic that China would emerge from World War I on a stronger footing with the Powers and that a revision of its treaties with them would result.[30] His views apparently were shared by other Chinese intellectuals and diplomats, who would soon adopt them as the foundation of an official Chinese position in negotiations concerning treaty revision. A far cry from the helplessness of the Manchus or the accommodation of Yuan Shih-k'ai, this approach reflected a new-found confidence and a sophisticated use of international law.

The Paris Peace Conference

The Republican government's first opportunity to seek a diplomatic resolution to the problem of foreign encroachment came at the 1919 Paris Peace Conference. Prior to the conference, no official measures had been taken to resolve Chinese concerns over extraterritoriality and leased or ceded territories. The Chinese government in 1917 had unilaterally abrogated its treaties with Germany, but that was a largely symbolic move under the circumstances of World War I, and it had no real effect on conditions in China. The Chinese had good reason to expect that the issue of foreign presence would be looked upon in a different light at the end of the war, however. They had been formal allies with the war's victors, thus earning a seat at the Versailles negotiating table and a position of respect that they had not previously enjoyed. As Tyau wrote, perhaps a bit optimistically, "China is no longer the negligible quantity which men used to know before the fateful days of August 1914."[31] Furthermore, in light of the attention given national autonomy and territorial integrity in President Woodrow Wilson's "Fourteen Points," the Chinese were hopeful of gaining a more sympathetic ear on the issue of sovereignty than they had in the past. The Chinese diplomat V. K. Wellington Koo had met with Wilson in Washington before the conference and had been assured of American support for at least some of the Chinese appeals. In Paris, Koo received further assurance that the American delegation would attempt to persuade the other powers to support the Chinese case.[32]

The Chinese delegation brought to Paris a long list of issues over which it sought redress. By 1915, eighteen countries had acquired special rights, privileges and territories in China. At the center of Chinese concerns was the "Shandong Question," the extensive territorial, mining, railroad and extraterritorial rights enjoyed in Shandong Province by foreign countries, especially Japan.

The Paris Conference was to be a major disappointment, however. Even before the conference began, there was an embarrassing dispute between the Beijing government and its KMT-led rival government based in Canton over the selection of a representative delegation. In Paris, Chinese participation was restricted. The delegation was permitted only two seats at the conference and allowed to appear before the Council of Ten or the Council of Four only by invitation.[33] In all, Chinese delegates were granted only three opportunities to present their case.

The main elements of the Chinese position at Paris were outlined in a document called "Questions for Readjustment," which spelled out clearly for the first time the Chinese argument for recovery of territorial sovereignty. Appealing to the Wilsonian tenets of "justice, equality and respect for the sovereignty of nations," the Chinese delegation requested that "all hindrances to China's free development be removed in conformity with the principles of territorial integrity, political independence and economic autonomy which appertain to every state."[34] Though the term "unequal treaties" had not yet entered the Chinese political lexicon, formal claims were made against "treaties or agreements made with China under circumstances precluding the free exercise of her will." All of these, the delegation's presentation said, served to hinder trade, threaten peace, and most important, seriously injure China's territorial integrity and political independence.[35] Based on these considerations, the Chinese government made several requests that reflected a more hopeful than realistic assessment of China's position at the talks:

> . . . the Chinese Government hope that the interested Powers will, out of their sincere regard for the sovereign rights of China and the common interests of all nations having trade relations with her, make a declaration, each for itself, to the effect that they have not any sphere of influence or interest in the Republic of China, nor intend to claim any; and that they are prepared to undertake a revision of such treaties, agreements, notes or contracts previously concluded with her as have conferred or may be

constructed to have conferred, on them, respectively, reserved territorial advantages or preferential rights or privileges to create spheres of influence or interest impairing the sovereign rights of China.[36]

The Chinese delegates did not lodge a request for the return of Hong Kong at Versailles, but they made several statements regarding leased territories, insisting on China's retention of sovereignty over them. "Though the exercise of administrative rights over the territory leased is relinquished by China to the lessee power during the period of the lease, the sovereignty of China over them is reserved in all cases . . . it appears clear that the leased territories remain part of Chinese territory, though encumbered with certain restrictions in regard to the exercise of administrative rights therein by the territorial sovereign."[37] Moreover, the Chinese diplomats argued, the original justification for acquiring leaseholds had disappeared. The Powers had sought to lease territories in order to preserve a balance of power in China among themselves, but such a balance was no longer necessary. It was on those grounds that China, for the first time, called for the return of leased territories:

> As prolongation of the foreign control over the leased territories constitutes a continual lordship, whose injurious effects tend from day to day to increase, the Chinese government feel in duty bound to ask for restitution of these territories, with the assurance that, in making their proposal, they are conscious of, and prepared to undertake, such obligations as the relinquishment of control may equitably entail on them as regards the protection of rights of property-owners therein and administration of the territories thus restored to the complete control of China.[38]

For all their eloquence and pledged righteousness, Chinese appeals at Versailles were never destined to receive serious consideration. Before the conference began, Britain and France had pledged secretly to support Japan's policies toward China, including the granting of former German concessions to the Japanese, and their combined efforts managed to stonewall Chinese requests.[39] China was allowed to present its "Questions for Readjustment" to the conference, but no action was taken on them. In addition to the British-French-Japanese conspiracy to deny Chinese appeals, the allies apparently felt that the Chinese had misinterpreted the purpose of the conference, which was to draft a peace settlement with the Central Powers, not to consider broader Chinese concerns.[40] As he had promised, President Wilson attempted to argue on behalf of the Chinese, but under the circumstances his efforts were of little real value.

The Chinese delegation expressed its disappointment at the conference's outcome by refusing to sign the Treaty of Versailles. In Beijing, the response to the conference was severe. On May 4, students marched in protest, sparking a powerful anti-imperialist, pro-modernization social movement that eventually would penetrate all elements of Chinese society. The May Fourth Movement focused and organized Chinese nationalist sentiment, and its effects on China's struggle against imperialism were to be profound.

Issues Raised Again: The Washington Conference

The Chinese government gained an opportunity to compensate for the disappointment of Versailles at the Conference on the Limitation of Armaments and Pacific and Far Eastern Questions, known as the Washington Conference, held from November 1921 through February 1922. Planned and organized by the United States, the conference was lauded by observers as an inspired attempt to apply Wilsonian principles of national self-determination to the postwar Far East. However, the American hosts were at least as interested in curbing Japan's military expansion and in securing a stable environment in East Asia in which to take advantage of China's "Open Door" trade policies.

The conference was divided into two major committees that dealt with separate sets of issues: the Committee on Limitation of Armament and the Committee on Pacific and Far Eastern Questions. The latter dealt almost exclusively with Chinese concerns, which centered on treaty and territorial issues. Wunsz King wrote, "Indeed it looked as though the formidable collection of unequal treaties and other related matters had been brought to Washington for thorough review or abrogation."[41]

The Chinese delegation numbered well over a hundred persons, all of whom represented the Beijing government, since the rival government at Canton had refused to participate. It was led by Dr. Sao-ke Alfred Sze, ambassador to Washington, assisted by Dr. V. K. Wellington Koo, ambassador to Great Britain and Dr. Chung-hui Wang, chief justice of the Chinese Supreme Court. On November 16, 1921, at the first meeting of the Committee on Pacific and Far Eastern Questions, Dr. Sze presented China's case, which amounted to a statement of principles, known since as China's "Ten Points."[42]

The arguments presented in the Ten Points, not surprisingly, were similar to those made at Versailles and shared the same focus on Shandong. The Chinese delegates called for an end to foreign domination of their country but emphasized their willingness to act responsibly and to cooperate with the Powers. They requested that other countries "respect and observe the territorial integrity and political and administrative independence of the Chinese Republic." While the main focus of these arguments was extraterritorial rights, the Chinese conception of "territorial integrity" referred to several kinds of arrangements, including spheres of interest, foreign settlements, foreign concessions and leased territories, all of which restricted China's authority to administer territory that fell within its own boundaries. In that regard, the Chinese delegation issued a direct appeal:

> All special rights, privileges, immunities or commitments, whatever their character or contractual basis, claimed by any of the Powers in or relating to China are to be declared, and all such or future claims not so made known, are to be deemed null and void. The rights, privileges, immunities and commitments, now known or to be declared, are to be examined with a view to determining their scope and validity and, if valid, to harmonizing them with one another and with the principles declared by this conference. . . . Immediately, or as soon as circumstances will permit, existing limitations upon China's political, jurisdictional and administrative freedom of action are to be removed.[43]

The Chinese had reason to be more hopeful of success in Washington than in Paris. Unlike Versailles, where Chinese requests were considered irrelevant to the peace treaty, one of the Washington Conference's goals was to give Chinese questions a thorough hearing. The Chinese position was further supported by Article 19 of the League of Nations Covenant, which encouraged states to free themselves from treaty obligations that had been imposed on them. It was in this spirit that Dr. Wang, at the Committee's sixth meeting, asked the Powers to set a date on which they would surrender all extraterritorial rights in China.[44]

The Chinese delegation was to achieve only limited success, however. Dr. Wang's request was sidestepped by an agreement to establish a committee that would consider the problem after the conference had adjourned. The most important result of the conference was a compromise agreement concerning Japanese withdrawal from Shandong. The port city of Qingdao, colonized by Germany and granted to Japan at Versailles, was returned to Chinese sovereignty, and an agreement was reached with the British that would eventually lead to their withdrawal from Weihaiwei. The status of the other leased territories, including Hong Kong's New Territories, was left unchanged. In the Nine-Power Treaty signed at the conference, the Powers agreed to a resolution which, without solving the problem of existing treaties, pledged to "respect the sovereignty, the independence, and the territorial and administrative integrity of China." It promised to give China an opportunity to develop a stable government, which the powers claimed was a prerequisite to returning tariff autonomy and jurisdictional rights, and in the meantime to refrain from making further encroachments on Chinese territory.[45]

As at Versailles, the Chinese delegation in Washington made a specific claim against leased territories. Dr. Koo asserted that, even if administrative rights had temporarily been forfeited, China retained sovereignty.[46] He pointed out that the existence of leased territories had "greatly prejudiced China's territorial and administrative integrity," especially since the leased territories were located at strategic points along China's coast, and that the logic of maintaining a balance among foreign powers in China had disappeared. Therefore, "In the interest not only of China, but of all nations, and especially with a view to the peace of the Far East, the Chinese delegation asks for the annulment or an early termination of these leases."[47] At the very least, he argued, the leaseholds should be demilitarized—their forts dismantled—pending termination of the leases.

The Chinese considered Hong Kong Island and Kowloon to be special cases and did not raise them for discussion in Washington. As ceded territories, they had been placed outside China's jurisdiction. Not until later, when the Chinese began to apply the notion of "unequal treaties," did they demand the return of the entire colony. The New Territories, however, was included among the leases discussed in Washington. But the British delegation argued that the New Territories was in a class of its own because it was required for the protection of Hong Kong Island rather than the maintenance of a broader balance of power. The Chinese conceded to the British on this point but indicated that they would continue to seek the return of the New Territories in the future. Dr. Koo explained the Chinese position:

> As to the leased territory of Kowloon, leased to Great Britain, much is to be said for the importance of Hong Kong to the trade of nations, and for the way in which its facilities are made accessible to the traders of the world, and while there may be a necessity to provide for the protection of the Hong Kong Harbor in the interests of such trade, the retention of Kowloon may not necessarily be, in the view of the Chinese delegation, the sole solution of this problem.[48]

The Chinese case presented in Washington also took a further step toward an argument against "unequal treaties." In requesting that the treaties resulting from Japan's Twenty-One Demands be annulled, Dr. Wang argued that "the Chinese Government and the Chinese people have always regarded these agreements as peculiar in themselves by reason of the circumstances under which they had been negotiated, and that the conditions arising under them were only *de facto* and without any legal recognition on the part of China." He continued, "Because of the essential injustice of these provisions, the Chinese delegation . . . has felt itself in duty bound to present to the conference . . . the question as to the equity and justice of these agreements and therefore as to their fundamental validity."[49] Though the question of legal validity in this context was not hotly debated in Washington, the development of this argument at this early stage is significant. In the coming years it was to become a major element of the Chinese position on Hong Kong.

More Dashed Hopes:
The Committee on Extraterritoriality

The Chinese delegation left Washington in February 1922 having achieved no real change in the extraterritoriality regime or the status of leased territories. But it carried with it the promise of another opportunity to state its case, since the conference had agreed to establish a commission to investigate and report on extraterritoriality and the administration of justice in China. The commission originally was scheduled to meet within three months of the close of the conference. In April, however, the Chinese requested a postponement until the fall of 1923. A series of delays followed, first as the Chinese prepared for the commission's investigation and then as the Powers tried to determine whether the Beijing government, which continued to enjoy diplomatic recognition, was stable enough to merit a reevaluation of the extraterritoriality regime. The commission finally convened in Beijing four years late, on January 12, 1926.

The list of issues on which the commission was to render an opinion, drafted by the United States Department of State, included foreign courts, the status of foreign nationals and other extraterritorial rights. In a memo to the commission, the Chinese insisted that the scope of their enquiry also include "special areas," such as leased territories. But the Powers' representatives refused, even over further Chinese appeals. They argued that such issues should be handled through diplomatic channels, since they were political and diplomatic in nature rather than juridical.[50]

As in the past, Chinese arguments before the commission emphasized sovereignty and administrative integrity. They also continued to be couched in accommodative language. There was no mention of "unequal treaties" (though the term by now had been used elsewhere), only "unwarranted interpretations of treaties." Their request for a "fundamental readjustment of China's relations with the Powers" included a promise to negotiate new treaties that would replace the ones under discussion.[51] A June 1925 note from the Chinese Foreign Ministry to representatives of the Washington Conference participants appealed to material instead of moral interests, arguing that diplomatic relations and trade would both improve if extraterritoriality were abolished. A Foreign Ministry representative explained that the note was drafted not only to present China's case but also to show Beijing's willingness to proceed in a congenial manner, "consonant with principles of international law."[52]

One of those principles was *rebus sic stantibus*, which by 1926 had become a prominent aspect of the Chinese approach to treaty revision. The Beijing government in 1926 argued that China's domestic circumstances had changed so dramatically since the Qing government signed the treaties that their terms could no longer be considered appropriate either to China's internal situation or to its relations with other countries: ". . . the change has affected the political, social, and economic life of the country, so that what appeared to be feasible seventy or eighty years ago can no longer be regarded as tenable."[53]

The Commission found such appeals unconvincing, however. It had come to China largely to determine whether the Beijing government exercised sufficient administrative control over the country to warrant termination of extraterritorial rights, but found little evidence of such control. Its final report recommended no major changes in the extraterritoriality system. Officially, the weak and fractured Chinese government in Beijing expressed disappointment, along with hope that the Powers at some point in the future would see fit to return to China all the full rights of a sovereign nation.[54] Yet the message surely was clear to both the Beijing and Canton governments, that China would recover its full territorial sovereignty only when it could stand as a unified nation, on equal diplomatic footing with the Powers.

Bilateral Negotiations

Though the Paris Peace Conference, the Washington Conference and the Extraterritoriality Commission represented the major international forums for discussion of treaty issues, the Beijing government also took its own steps in the 1920s to reach bilateral agreements with the Powers. In April 1926, officials in Beijing informed the Belgian government of their desire to negotiate the revision of a treaty which dealt mostly with tariff privileges and jurisdictional rights, once again basing their case on *rebus sic stantibus*. After nine months of debate, including an appeal to the Permanent Court of International Justice, the two governments agreed on terms for a new treaty which included Belgian rendition of its concession at Tianjin. Similar appeals were made, with some success, to the French, Japanese, Spanish and American governments in late 1926 and early 1927.[55] Great Britain, after considerable Foreign Office and Colonial Office debate, disclaimed all intentions to perpetuate imperialism in China in a "Christmas message" on December 26, 1926, and the following January began actual work on treaty revision. No specific reference was made to Hong Kong Island, Kowloon or the New Territories, which the British were unwilling to return. They were more inclined to negotiate over extraterritorial rights and the strategically less important territory of Weihaiwei. The Chinese government, on the other hand, always included the New Territories lease among agreements that it proposed to abrogate. It would be some years before an opportunity would come to press those claims.

Growing Demands Against Unequal Treaties

China's attempts in the international arena to abrogate or revise its treaties with the Powers in part reflect the growth of nationalist sentiment, especially after 1919. As the product of an antiforeignism that had been growing since at least the middle of the nineteenth century, the Chinese nationalist movement targeted the obvious examples of foreign exploitation that existed within Chinese territory, including control over territories, railroads, mines and customs operations, stationing of foreign troops on Chinese soil, and the acquisition of extraterritorial rights. A compromise that allowed foreigners to remain in China and continue to enjoy favorable commercial terms would probably have been acceptable to Chinese elites, but the call for China's leaders to make at least some progress had grown strong. The Chinese government explained in a statement to the Extraterritoriality Commission: "If, in those early days of intercourse with foreign countries, the matter of relinquishing jurisdiction over aliens in China was viewed by the government of the day with complacency, today it would be difficult, if not impossible, to persuade an awakened nation to adopt the same viewpoint."[56]

This change in attitude is reflected in the increasing use of the term "unequal treaty." References to the principle of equality in international relations or to the injustice of imposing treaties with force began to appear after 1915. But the first known reference to unequal treaties appeared in a KMT declaration dated January 1, 1923. The declaration condemned the Qing government for concluding "unequal treaties" and pledged to "make efforts to rectify [those unequal] treaties so as to restore China's free and equal status on the international level."[57] A year later, the KMT's First National Convention declared that "all unequal treaties . . . should be cancelled and new treaties based upon mutual equality and respect for sovereignty should be reconcluded." Sun Yat-sen's will, dated March 11, 1925, ordered that "the abolition of unequal treaties should be carried into effect with the least possible delay." And the Beijing government's first official use of the term was in November

1926, in reference to the Sino-Belgian Treaty of 1865.[58] By the time the Nationalists formally established their national government at Nanjing in 1928, the term was widely used by both Chinese and foreigners to refer to a long list of treaties.

The term "unequal treaty" expressed both the passionate and rational aspects of popular Chinese attitudes toward foreign encroachment. It reflected a popular bitterness toward the cruel mistreatment China had received from foreigners, while at the same time appealing to the foreigners' own sense of fairness. The term encompassed the moral aspect of China's pleas for treaty abrogation, which said that using force to gain rights and territory in China had been wrong, and the legal element, which argued that accepted tenets of international law supported the Chinese case for treaty revision. The concept of unequal treaties thus became a rallying point for anti-imperialist sentiment in China.

As use of the term grew during the 1920s, so did the intensity of popular demands for the recovery of China's territorial integrity. The years following the Paris Peace Conference had seen an unprecedented display of popular antiforeignism in demonstrations, strikes, boycotts and riots, directed especially against the Japanese and British. These popular movements, involving intellectuals, students and workers, provided convincing evidence to foreigners in China, and in a most painful fashion to the British in Hong Kong, that a new era in Chinese politics had begun.

Relations with the Colony

Despite increased attention devoted to issues concerning unequal treaties in this period, Chinese leaders were able to take only limited measures against foreign interests. The country was fractured politically and militarily, with different regions ruled by competing warlords. When the Extraterritoriality Commission met in Beijing, its deliberations were delayed by fighting over control of the city. The "central government" in Beijing therefore was more concerned with preserving its own fragile authority than with pursuing nationalist goals.

Though the Beijing government continued to enjoy formal British recognition until the KMT established national control in 1928, its authority did not extend to Canton. Hong Kong's political relations with the mainland centered on the KMT organization in Canton and on the rival government there, which Sun Yat-sen established formally in 1917 but whose existence was under constant challenge until Chiang Kai-shek was able to assert his dominance in 1926. Canton's relationship with the colony in this period demonstrates an increasing tension between the KMT's willingness to allow British Hong Kong to prosper and its need, for reasons of domestic support, to wave the anti-imperialist banner. This tension, combined with the nationwide antiforeign movement and developments in Hong Kong itself, resulted in the colony's first major antigovernment disturbances. The events of the 1920s in Hong Kong awakened the KMT leadership to the power of the antiforeign issue as a means of gaining popular support and alerted the British rulers in Hong Kong to their own vulnerability.

The 1922 Seamen's Strike

Hong Kong's economy experienced a downturn in the years following World War I. The shipping industry sagged, prices rose and shortages of commodities and foodstuffs became common. Partly in response to these circumstances and partly in response to political activism on the mainland, Hong Kong began to experience serious labor unrest. The Chinese Seamen's Union Strike of 1922, the first major strike in Hong Kong's history, lasted fifty-two days and at its height involved 120,000 workers, including nearly all the seamen in the colony and sympathy strikers in various other industries.[59]

Labor unrest had emerged in Hong Kong in 1920, when the Machinists Union held out successfully for substantial wage increases. Inspired by this success and by increased labor organization on the mainland, Hong Kong's workers began to organize in opposition to oppressive wage rates and working conditions. The colony's Chinese seamen suffered from particularly harsh circumstances. Wages were extremely low, and what little buying power they brought was eroded by postwar inflation. The seamen were also held hostage to an oppressive contract hiring system by which the contractor could retain as a commission up to eighty percent of a worker's wages. In 1921, the Hong Kong Seamen's Union was established with the immediate goal of seeking redress on these two issues. After initial requests for wage increases were denied by the Hong Kong government, the Seamen's Union declared a strike in January 1922.[60]

What began as an economic issue soon became politicized. In response to the strike, the Hong Kong government declared a state of emergency and sealed the border. In early March, after several weeks had passed with no sign of compromise on the government's part, a large group of strikers decided to return to Canton. Travelling on foot, the group numbered about two thousand as it reached Shatin in the New Territories, where the seamen met a military cordon established by Hong Kong government authorities. Lacking the passes necessary to proceed past Shatin under the state of emergency, the strikers attempted to break through the cordon. The soldiers fired a warning shot, followed by several volleys that killed three strikers and wounded eight others. The event quickly became known among Chinese in Hong Kong and Canton as the "Shatin Massacre."[61] It galvanized anti-British sentiment and helped bring about the end of the strike, as the Hong Kong government shortly thereafter agreed to upgrade the seamen's wage scale and abolish the contract system. The harbor returned to normal, though the Seamen's Strike had altered the relationship between Chinese workers and the Hong Kong government in a manner that was to have broader implications for the colony.

Reaction to the strike among officials and politicians in Canton reflects the tension that would later become a central element of the China–Hong Kong relationship. Kuomintang leaders in Canton were inclined to support the strikers, both to express their opposition to British colonialism and to nurture the support of workers in Canton and Hong Kong. The KMT provided office space to the strike's organizers, held a reception for the strikers and provided crucial financial support that amounted to one-third of total strike expenses. This support paid immediate dividends, as 20,000 new members, half of them seamen, joined the KMT during the strike.[62]

But key KMT officials, especially those on its right wing, were reluctant to appear too supportive of the strike. The KMT attempted to keep its financial assistance secret, and a Kuomintang official sent a letter to Hong Kong's *South China Morning Post* to refute publicly reports that it had hosted some of the strikers' representatives in Canton.[63] The KMT's lack of enthusiasm reflects concern over the economic damage an extended strike would bring to Canton's own businessmen, as well as the close ties that conservative KMT members and Cantonese gentry shared with British traders, who suffered most from the interruption of cargo traffic through Hong Kong.[64]

The fledgling Military Government at Canton, controlled by the conservative provincial governor and military commander, Ch'en Chiung-ming, who was on good terms with the British in Hong Kong, responded even more cautiously. The government took no official position on the strike, persistently denied rumors that government officials had aided the strikers, and called for a quick settlement. Sun Yat-sen, the government's nominal leader, was in Guangxi preparing a military campaign when the strike broke out. He was sympathetic with the seamen's demands and early in the strike sent them an encouraging telegram. But he later sent a telegram urging the strikers to settle, even short of total victory. After the strike ended, he retreated from his support for it: "As far as the suggestion that I supported the strike in order to damage British interests, I absolutely repudiate it." The Shatin Massacre provided a convenient pretext to take a strong stand in favor of the

strikers, but the Canton government declined, deferring to a Hong Kong `
government inquiry instead.[65] Reestablished at Canton only a year earlier
after a two-year forced absence, the Military Government hoped to gain
financial assistance and diplomatic recognition through the colony. Sun
Yat-sen and others in the government were therefore anxious to avoid
offending the British in Hong Kong.

The 1925–1926 Strike-Boycott

The 1922 Seamen's Strike had a major economic impact in Hong
Kong, but its more lasting effects were political. The strike inspired
labor unrest in other parts of China and demonstrated to the KMT and
CCP the advantages of organizing and recruiting workers, particularly
by relying on antiforeign themes. These effects became apparent in the
Canton–Hong Kong Strike-Boycott of 1925–1926, which dramatically
exceeded its predecessor in scale, in the extent of Canton's official
involvement, and in the threat it posed to the British livelihood in Hong
Kong.

On May 30, 1925, police officers under British command in Shanghai
fired on a large group of antiforeign demonstrators. The "May Thirtieth
Incident" set off a massive wave of antiforeign strikes and boycotts
across coastal China. In Canton, the KMT decided to strike against Hong
Kong and the international settlement at Shameen, a small island in the
Pearl River at Canton. The Seamen's Union again led the way, declaring
a strike on June 18 that was joined the following day by most other
unions. On June 23, the strikers organized a demonstration in Canton
that drew ten thousand people. As the demonstrators marched along
the river opposite Shameen, a shot rang out (its source remains a matter
of dispute) and British and French troops on the island opened fire on
the crowd, killing 52 people and wounding 117. After this "Shameen
Massacre," the Strike-Boycott intensified. A boycott of all goods and
ships travelling via Hong Kong was instituted. By the end of June, the
colony and its harbor had come to a standstill, the government had
declared a state of emergency and essential services were being provided
by volunteers. By early July, 200,000 workers had joined the strike and
its disastrous economic effects in Hong Kong, most notably a huge drop
in trade, could already be felt.[66] The total number of strikers would
later reach 250,000.

The 1925–1926 Strike-Boycott was much more overtly political than
its precursor in 1922. The strikers' demands included work-related items,
such as a minimum wage, an eight-hour day, workers' insurance and
collective bargaining arrangements, but they also called for freedom of
speech and of publication, racial equality and extension of the franchise.[67]

Participants in the June 23 demonstration marched to such slogans as "Down with the imperialists" and "Abolish all unequal treaties." A series of propaganda telegrams sent by Seamen's Union members to national and foreign labor organizations expressed their resolve "to lay down our lives in the struggle against Imperialism and Capitalism . . . All unequal treaties must be abolished . . . never will [Hong Kong workers] allow the imperialists within our territory freely to crush us."[68]

Unlike the 1922 strike, the Strike-Boycott also enjoyed substantial support from Canton. The KMT's First National Congress in January 1924 had called for the abolition of all unequal treaties, including those concerning leased territories, as had the Party's Manifesto on the Northern Expedition in September.[69] And while the specific nature of the KMT's role has been disputed, it is clear that KMT officials worked closely with the two organizations directing the strike: the Canton–Hong Kong Strike Committee and the All-China General Union. The CCP, having joined with the KMT in 1924 as part of a United Front strategy to gain national authority, was also heavily involved in directing the strike; two of its top leaders, Lin Wei-min and Su Chao-cheng, had become CCP members since their first strike efforts in 1922. The strike's organizers ran a tightly controlled and extremely effective operation, with highly disciplined pickets and an internal police unit that enforced the strike and boycott.

During the first part of the sixteen-month strike, the KMT stood firmly in support of the workers. Liao Chung-k'ai, a leader of the party's dominant left wing and an enthusiastic supporter of the strike, addressed a meeting of the Strikers' Delegates Congress in August 1925, claiming that "Hong Kong is our first target in the struggle against imperialism . . . we must break Hong Kong."[70] The KMT's Second National Convention in January 1926, which affirmed the dominance of the party's left wing, strongly endorsed the Strike-Boycott, calling Hong Kong workers the "vanguard of the revolution."[71] There were pockets of conservatism in the party as well. Indeed, some members initially had urged that the strike be limited to three days. Those voices were drowned out, however, by the resounding popular response to the Shameen Incident.[72]

As in 1922, the KMT's government at Canton found itself in a difficult diplomatic position. Its support for the strikers is reflected in the substantial financial assistance it provided, amounting to more than half of the total strike funds. The government also moved to begin development of the Whampoa docks, a strategy that Sun Yat-sen had envisioned several years earlier as a means to weaken Hong Kong's grip on South China's trade.[73] But the Nationalist Government also tried to maintain a facade of neutrality that revealed its reluctance to see the Strike-Boycott go too far. In a meeting with Hong Kong Governor Stubbs in early June 1925, Foreign Minister C. C. Wu and Sun Fo, Sun Yat-sen's son, expressed their sentiments of goodwill toward the colony and promised to try to prevent "untoward actions" there.[74] Mikhail Borodin, the Comintern's adviser to the government at Canton, explained in 1926 that one of his goals following the Shameen Incident was to restrain the reactions of Canton's residents and "keep them from doing things that might bring on a war with the West."[75]

The Canton government's ambivalence ended in the spring of 1926. In March, Chiang Kai-shek placed Canton under military control and ordered the strike headquarters searched. Though he later called this move against the strike leadership a misunderstanding, Chiang had clearly signalled a change in direction. In late April, officials in Canton drew up draft proposals for a settlement. In May, Chiang established his firm control over the KMT, and its Central Executive Committee agreed to seek negotiations with the Hong Kong government to end the strike. At the end of May, Eugene Chen (Ch'en Yu-jen) was appointed minister of foreign affairs and directed to open negotiations, the Nationalist government's first public acknowledgement of its involvement in the strike.

Negotiations began in July, one week after Chiang launched his Northern Expedition to bring the country under Nationalist control. They quickly reached an impasse, however, over the issue of compensation to the strikers, and the strike tightened again. In September, however, the government decided to declare an end to the strike unilaterally, effective October 10, the anniversary of the 1911 Revolution. The Northern Expedition had reached the Yangtze River valley, and Chiang apparently wanted to insure British cooperation there, as well as to secure his base in Canton against further disruption. Under these circumstances, the original aspirations of the strikers and the movement to oppose imperialism in the Canton Delta took a back seat to the KMT's more immediate political goals.

The Strike-Boycott held important lessons for the KMT and for the British in Hong Kong. It revealed that labor organization, especially when combined with antiforeign agitation, represented a potent means of gaining political support. Hong Kong, whose economy suffered huge losses during the strike while Canton's economy grew slightly, was shown to be extremely vulnerable to organized Chinese opposition. When they enjoyed official support, the strike's organizers were able to control its implementation tightly and to persuade recalcitrant workers in Hong Kong to join the cause. The Hong Kong government's attempts to circumvent the strike by bringing in workers from other Chinese cities met with little success.

The British position was strengthened by two factors, however. One was the high level of economic and social integration between Canton and Hong Kong, which meant that wealthy Cantonese appreciated the extent to which their own fortunes were tied up with Hong Kong's. The second was the limited nature of the KMT's aims regarding the colony. Most KMT officials recognized that the British presence in Hong Kong represented an affront to China's territorial integrity and were willing to use popular anti-British sentiment to their political advantage. However, elimination of British rule itself was not an immediate goal. Foreign Minister Eugene Chen explained in June 1926 that the Chinese were "against British institutions in China that are unjust to the Chinese, not against Englishmen as such in China or elsewhere."[76]

Chinese Nationalism and Hong Kong

The new Chinese nationalism that took on considerable force in the 1920s represented in principle a serious threat to British authority in Hong Kong. Indeed, the two major strikes that took place in the colony demonstrate the powerful impact that the new militant antiforeignism in Chinese politics could have on its economy and lifestyle. Hong Kong was an obvious target for this movement, both because it was a glaring example of colonialism and because of the Comintern's decision in the mid-1920s to focus on Great Britain as China's major anti-imperialist target. Still, the British position in Hong Kong seems never to have been in real danger. Anti-British activism in Canton depended on support from the KMT and, to a lesser extent, the CCP. While the left wing of the KMT was willing to cause far more disruption in Hong Kong than the conservatives who ultimately retained power, neither group was willing or able to challenge British rule seriously. Chinese politicians recognized, particularly after the May Thirtieth and Shameen Incidents, that antiforeign sentiment had become a galvanizing political force that could be used to gain popular support. Nevertheless, they also recognized that the risks associated with an outright challenge to the British position in Hong Kong were unacceptable.

The most obvious reason for this reluctance was the overwhelming superiority of the British military forces. Any attempt to take Hong Kong by force almost surely would have ended in military disaster and political embarrassment. The presence of British gunboats in Canton was a strong reminder of this fact, and it was reinforced when they were employed as threats, once during the Shameen Incident and once near the end of the Strike-Boycott.

The Canton government's capacity to challenge Hong Kong's status was further constrained by its own instability. The Nationalist government faced internal divisions and external opposition that sought to force it from Canton. Even after Chiang Kai-shek consolidated power in his own hands in the spring of 1926, his attention was turned to the more pressing concern of undertaking the Northern Expedition. The question of the British position in Hong Kong could be left for later.

The governments at Canton and Beijing were also cautious about the manner in which they pursued claims against foreign powers. Chinese diplomatic statements from this period reveal a concern with projecting a responsible image in the international arena. Appeals for the return of territory reflect a respect for diplomatic convention and accepted principles of international law. Requests for abrogation of old treaties were accompanied with promises of new ones. Chinese officials attempted repeatedly to prove to skeptical foreign governments that they were prepared to assume the full rights and responsibilities of a sovereign nation.

Chinese officials, particularly in Canton, also appreciated the benefits that the colony provided by virtue of its location and independent status. Even at this early stage, Hong Kong showed signs of becoming a "door to the West," as it later would become known. In a 1923 speech at Hong Kong University, Sun Yat-sen, who was banned from the colony from 1896 to 1911 because of his political activities there, recalled the lessons he had learned while studying medicine in Hong Kong:

> I compared Heungshan [his birthplace] with Hong Kong, and although they are only fifty miles apart, the difference of the government oppressed me very much [sic]. Afterwards I saw the outside world, and I began to wonder how it was that foreigners, that Englishmen, could do so much as they had done, for example, with the barren rock of Hong Kong within seventy or eighty years, while in four thousand years China had no place like Hong Kong. . . . My fellow students. You and I have studied in this English university. We must learn by English examples. We must carry this English example of good government to every part of China.[77]

Canton shared close political, economic and social ties with its neighboring colony. The local Republican government formed in 1912 not only turned to Hong Kong for advice, but also included among its members several Hong Kong Chinese, one of whom was a British subject.[78] The two economies were linked closely through Hong Kong's role as the chief port of South China and through personal ties between Canton and Hong Kong elites. Most Chinese in Hong Kong had relatives in Canton and travel across the border was frequent.

The two were integrated in other ways as well. Refugees from the mainland found a safe haven in Hong Kong, as they would decades later. Between 1911 and 1913, 40,000 people took refuge in the territory, including the former viceroy and governor-general of Canton and their families. In 1915, the Chinese vice-minister for foreign affairs expressed his appreciation to Hong Kong authorities for their treatment of political refugees from China.[79] Sun Yat-sen escaped to Hong Kong on a British gunboat when he was forced from Canton in June 1922. The colony also became a convenient location for political organization and fund-raising, so that by the late 1920s one Hong Kong government official called it "a base for intrigue in the neighboring republic."[80]

British Hong Kong also provided the mainland with important economic benefits. One of the first acts of the new Republican government was to send a delegation to Hong Kong seeking money and advice, both of which were supplied in abundance. In the 1920s Hong Kong was the most important shipping center in the Far East, the railway terminus for South China and a terminus for American, British and Chinese air services. More than thirty percent of China's total trade passed through the colony,[81] which was the distribution and financial center for all of South China. When China's internal political and economic situations were unstable, Hong Kong continued to provide reliable service. In an official government statement regarding the 1922 Seamen's Strike, Foreign Minister Chen emphasized these ties: "If the government has any interest in the matter, it is and must be for the speedy settlement of the dispute. As long as Hong Kong is and continues to be Canton's ocean-gateway, the latter cannot but suffer from any dispute which seriously affects Hong Kong as a great shipping center."[82]

Thus there were important reasons that Hong Kong remained in British hands while, just across the border, anti-imperialist sentiment approached a fever pitch. China's nationalist movement in the 1920s did have a major effect on life in the colony, but its impact was limited by political considerations on the mainland. In this respect, the disturbances of the 1920s in Hong Kong foreshadowed those of 1967.[83] In the years following the Nationalist government's move from Canton to Nanjing, Chinese efforts to recover territory and dismantle the system of extraterritoriality, begun so tentatively after the First World War, would achieve their first successes. Yet Hong Kong, caught in a web of competing Chinese policy goals, would continue to thrive.

Notes

1. Chiang Kai-shek, *China's Destiny*, Wang Chung-hui, trans. (N.Y.: DeCapo Press, 1976): 17.

2. Peter Wesley-Smith, *Unequal Treaty 1898–1997: China, Great Britain and Hong Kong's New Territories* (Hong Kong: Oxford University Press, 1980): 57–

66; R. G. Groves, "Militia, Market and Lineage: Chinese Resistance to the Occupation of Hong Kong's New Territories in 1899," *Journal of the Hong Kong Branch of the Royal Asiatic Society* 9 (1969): 42–59.

3. Jacques Gernet, *A History of Chinese Civilization* (Cambridge: Cambridge University Press, 1982): 601.

4. "Declaration of Policy by the President of China, October 10, 1913," in "Report of the Commission on Extraterritoriality in China," Sept. 16, 1926 (Washington, D.C.: Government Printing Office, 1926): 115.

5. Kuang-sheng Liao, *Antiforeignism and Modernization in China, 1860–1980* (Hong Kong: The Chinese University Press, 1984): 84–85.

6. "Hong Kong Original Correspondence," *Great Britain Colonial Office Papers*, CO 129/380, pp. 276–80.

7. *Colonial Office*, CO 129/380, p. 196.

8. *Colonial Office*, CO 129/380, pp. 46–48, 200.

9. *Colonial Office*, CO 129/388, p. 60.

10. *Colonial Office*, CO 129/380, p. 200.

11. *Colonial Office*, CO 129/378, p. 291.

12. *Colonial Office*, CO 129/378, p. 155.

13. *Colonial Office*, CO 129/380, p. 200.

14. *Colonial Office*, CO 129/388, p. 61.

15. *Colonial Office*, CO 129/385, p. 198.

16. *Colonial Office*, CO 129/392, p. 196.

17. *Colonial Office*, CO 129/388, p. 62.

18. *Colonial Office*, CO 129/380, p. 198, and CO 129/391, p. 35.

19. *Colonial Office*, CO 129/399, p. 341.

20. *Colonial Office*, CO 129/399, p. 349.

21. *Colonial Office*, CO 129/399, p. 513.

22. *Colonial Office*, CO 129/394, pp. 133–34.

23. *Colonial Office*, CO 129/405, p. 596.

24. John V. A. MacMurray, ed., *Treaties and Agreements With and Concerning China, 1894–1919* (N.Y.: Howard Fertig, 1973): 1236.

25. MacMurray, *Treaties*, 1215.

26. *Colonial Office*, CO 129/414, pp. 10–11.

27. Wen-Sze King, "The Lease Conventions Between China and the Foreign Powers: An Interpretation," *The Chinese Social and Political Science Review* 1, no. 4 (Dec. 1916): 24–36.

28. M. T. Z. Tyau, "China and the Peace Conference," *The Chinese Social and Political Science Review*, 2, no. 2 (June 1917): 22–54.

29. On competing definitions and the application of *rebus sic stantibus* in international law, see Arie E. David, *The Strategy of Treaty Termination: Lawful Breaches and Retaliations* (London: Yale University Press, 1975): 4–55.

30. M. T. Z. Tyau, "Diplomatic Relations Between China and the Powers, Since and Concerning, the European War," *The Chinese Social and Political Science Review* 2, no. 4 (Dec. 1917): 6–67.

31. M. T. Z. Tyau, "Diplomatic Relations," 42.

32. Wunsz King, *Woodrow Wilson, Wellington Koo and the China Question at the Paris Peace Conference* (Leyden: A. W. Sythoff, 1959): 5–8.

33. Wesley R. Fishel, *The End of Extraterritoriality in China* (N.Y.: Octagon Books, 1974): 36.

34. "Questions for Readjustment, Submitted by China to the Peace Conference," *The Chinese Social and Political Science Review*, vol. 1A, no. 1–2: 116.

35. "Questions for Readjustment," 117–19.

36. "Questions for Readjustment," 119.

37. "Questions for Readjustment," 144.

38. "Questions for Readjustment," 144–45.

39. Fishel, *Extraterritoriality*, 38.

40. Fishel, *Extraterritoriality*, 40.

41. Wunsz King, *China at the Washington Conference, 1921–1922* (N.Y.: St. John's University Press, 1963): 3.

42. King, *Washington Conference*, 2. For a complete list of the Ten Points, see King, *Washington Conference*, 62–63.

43. King, *Washington Conference*, 63.

44. King, *Washington Conference*, 52; Fariborz Nozari, *Unequal Treaties in International Law* (Stockholm: S. Byran Sundt and Co., 1971): 109.

45. Fishel, *Extraterritoriality*, 56. The Powers' reservations over Chinese political stability and unity were reflected in a London *Times* editorial prior to the Washington Conference that argued, "China, from the point of view of international relations is, in her present state, largely a fiction." See King, *Washington Conference*, 28.

46. Westel W. Willoughby, *Foreign Rights and Interests in China*, orig. pub. 1927 (Taipei: Ch'eng Wen Publishing Co., 1966): 184.

47. Willoughby, *Foreign Rights*, 485.

48. Willoughby, *Foreign Rights*, 490.

49. Willoughby, *Foreign Rights*, 233, 235.

50. Fishel, *Extraterritoriality*, 76, 113–14.

51. "Declaration and Memoranda by the Chinese Commissioner Presented to the Commission on Extraterritoriality" (London: His Majesty's Stationery Office, 1927): 13.

52. Fishel, *Extraterritoriality*, 91.

53. "Declaration and Memoranda," 1.

54. "Declaration and Memoranda," 15.

55. Fishel, *Extraterritoriality*, 127–39; *Foreign Relations of the United States*, 1927, vol. 2 (Washington, D.C.: Government Printing Office): 54.

56. "Declaration and Memoranda," 15.

57. Jerome Alan Cohen, ed., *China's Practice of International Law: Some Case Studies* (Cambridge: Harvard University Press, 1972): 245–46.

58. Cohen, *China's Practice*, 246–48.

59. G. B. Endacott, *A History of Hong Kong*, 2nd ed. (Hong Kong: Oxford University Press, 1977): 290; Jean Chesneaux, *The Chinese Labor Movement, 1919–1927* (Stanford: Stanford University Press, 1968): 184.

60. For details of the strike, see Ming K. Chan, *Labour and Empire: The Chinese Labour Movement in the Canton Delta, 1895–1927* (Ph.D. Dissertation, Stanford University, 1975): 268–85; John Earl Motz, *Great Britain, Hong Kong and Canton: The Canton–Hong Kong Strike and Boycott of 1925–1926* (Ph.D. Dissertation, Michigan State University, 1972): 10–20; John Young, "China's Role in Two Hong Kong Disturbances: A Scenario for the Future?," *Journal of Oriental Studies* 19, no. 2 (1981): 158–74; Rosemarie Lu Cee Chung, *A Study of the 1925–26 Canton Strike-Boycott* (M.A. Thesis, University of Hong Kong, 1969); 32–60; William Ayers, "The Hong Kong Strikes, 1920–1926," *Harvard Papers on China* 4 (1950): 101–15; Chesneaux. *Chinese Labor*, 180–85.

61. Chung, *Strike-Boycott*, 34–35; Motz, *Great Britain*, 17.

62. Chan, *Labour*, 294–95. Though the strike's two leaders later became Communists, in 1922 the CCP organization in Canton was too small to have an impact on the strike.

63. Chung, *Strike-Boycott*, 37.

64. Chesneaux, *Chinese Labor*, 183–84.

65. Chan, *Labour*, 290–93.

66. Chan, *Labour*, 308–14; Motz, *Great Britain*, 45–90; Young, "China's Role," 160–65; Chesneaux, *Chinese Labor*, 290–318.

67. Chesneaux, *Chinese Labor*, 291.

68. Chung, *Strike-Boycott*, 81, 92.

69. Liao, *Antiforeignism*, 82–83.

70. Young, "China's Role," 164.

71. Chung, *Strike-Boycott*, 306.

72. Chan, *Labour*, 311.

73. Chan, *Labour*, 317, 141.

74. Chung, *Strike-Boycott*, 78.

75. John McCook Roots, *Chou* (N.Y.: Doubleday and Co., 1978): 199–200.

76. Chung, *Strike-Boycott*, 289.

77. Quoted in H. G. W. Woodhead, "Shanghai and Hong Kong: A British View," *Foreign Affairs* 23 (Jan. 1945): 300.

78. *Colonial Office*, CO 129/380, p. 198.

79. *Colonial Office*, CO 129/428, p. 346.

80. *Colonial Office*, CO 129/403, pp. 7–9.

81. Chung, *Strike-Boycott*, 21.

82. Ayers, "Strikes," 115.

83. For an interesting comparison of the disturbances in 1925–1926 and 1967, see Young, "China's Role."

3

The Nationalist Government and the Struggle for Hong Kong's Return

Chiang Kai-shek's successful Northern Expedition in 1926–1927 and the subsequent establishment of a Nationalist government at Nanjing held important implications for the foreign presence in China. The Powers had for years argued that the political situation in China was not sufficiently stable and that no government commanded sufficient national authority to merit the renegotiation of treaties signed by the Manchus; in other words, the Chinese were unable to rule themselves. But Chiang Kai-shek, by establishing a government led by the right wing of the KMT, seriously debilitating his opposition and unifying, however tentatively, a significant portion of the country, had brought that argument into question. At least for a short time after 1928, the Nationalists were in a better position to demand abrogation or renegotiation of unequal treaties than any Chinese leadership had been since their signing.

In fact, in the years immediately following the establishment of their government at Nanjing, the Nationalists undertook a vigorous diplomatic campaign to abrogate the unequal treaties still in force. After the Japanese invasion of Manchuria in 1931, those efforts were suspended for ten years. Nevertheless, it was under the Nationalists' leadership that major agreements were reached with a number of countries, including the United States and Great Britain, to return territory and terminate special rights. The three treaties that leased and ceded Hong Kong to the British, however, slipped through the KMT's hands.

The Nanjing Government and Unequal Treaties

When Foreign Minister Huang Fu assumed office on February 16, 1928, he immediately announced the Nationalist government's desire to begin negotiations at the earliest possible date for the conclusion of new treaties with the Powers, "on the basis of equality and mutual respect

41

for territorial sovereignty."[1] This initiated a diplomatic campaign, known as the "rights recovery movement," that was considered crucial to putting China's international relations on solid ground. The Nationalist approach was to be firm in principle but cautious in application; foreigners' rights in China would not be forcefully terminated. A government declaration of June 1928 confirmed this approach:

> To realize its hope of a new state the Nationalist Government must put its international relations on a new basis. For 80 years China has been under the shackles of unequal treaties. These restrictions are a contravention of the principle in international law, of mutual respect and sovereignty and are not allowed by any sovereign state. . . . Now that the unification of China is being consummated we think the time is ripe for taking further steps and begin at once to negotiate—in accordance with diplomatic procedure—new treaties on a basis of complete equality and mutual respect for each other's sovereignty.[2]

As armies supporting Beijing retreated in the summer of 1928, the Nanjing government's claim to national authority was strengthened. In July the Foreign Ministry published a strongly-worded declaration against unequal treaties, calling them "the most pressing problem at the present time." The declaration listed three basic elements of Chinese policy: (1) all expired unequal treaties would be *ipso facto* abrogated, (2) interim regulations would be devised to deal with treaties that had expired without being replaced, and (3) steps would be taken to terminate existing unequal treaties and to conclude new ones.[3] This newly aggressive approach reflected the KMT's growing confidence in its own national leadership and its self-perception as the redeemer of China's territorial integrity.

In January 1929, the KMT adopted a program whose foreign policy statement adhered closely to these principles. Without mentioning Hong Kong's New Territories by name, it cited leasehold agreements specifically among the treaties that would require renegotiation. In December, the Chinese Foreign Ministry went one step further, issuing a mandate that for the first time, at least in form, unilaterally ended extraterritorial rights in China.[4]

But it was the National People's Convention of 1931 that produced the Nationalists' strongest policy statement on unequal treaties. Referring to the principles of sovereignty, justice and equality, the "Manifesto Concerning the Abrogation of Unequal Treaties" argued for abrogation on three grounds that echoed the reasoning presented at Paris and Washington: (1) a change in China's domestic circumstances and international position made *rebus sic stantibus* applicable under international law, (2) the unequal treaties were contrary to League of Nations principles, specifically Article 19 of its charter, which referred to "treaties which have become inapplicable," and they hindered the international struggle for racial equality and peace, and (3) China's administrative machinery had improved enough that China should be allowed to manage its own affairs. The conclusions it drew were unequivocal:

1. The Chinese people will not recognize all the past unequal treaties imposed by the Powers on China.
2. The National Government shall, in conformity with Dr. Sun Yat-sen's testamentary injunction, achieve with least possible delay China's equality and independence in the Family of Nations.[5]

As a statement of intent, the Manifesto, like earlier declarations, was ineffectual; certainly it posed no immediate threat to the British in Hong Kong. Nevertheless, the document reflects a more aggressive posture that the Nationalist government hoped to carry into negotiations concerning treaty revision. In light of the KMT's origins and early anti-imperialist orientation, such a posture is not surprising. Its leadership's commitment to the elimination of foreign exploitation, while less vigorous than the anti-imperialist bias the CCP would later display, nevertheless was genuine. In addition, the urban atmosphere of the 1920s in China, with its antiforeign demonstrations and strikes, had made the KMT's leadership starkly aware of the implications of the unequal treaty issue for the party's attempts to build popular support. One American close to KMT officials was reported to have told U.S. President Hoover that,

> while the present government might be considered a moderate government, whatever government might succeed it must of necessity take this [hard-line] stand on the question of extraterritoriality as there was plenty of sentiment in China among those actively interested in those matters to force any spokesman for China to take this stand. He stated that there was a large radical element in China which was using this as a whip to beat the present government with . . . whatever moderated desires might exist among individual Chinese minds, no government could expect to stand or carry on successfully in its work of stabilization that did not press this question. . . .

The American further explained that Chinese sentiment could no longer allow for gradual adjustments, as it might have a few years earlier. Only "immediate and unconditional surrender of extraterritorial rights" would suffice.[6]

What the Nationalist government promised in principle, however, it was not necessarily able to pursue in fact. Even after the promulgation of the strongly-worded Manifesto in 1931, which came after eighteen months of difficult treaty negotiations with foreign governments, no efforts were made to compel foreigners to obey Chinese laws or submit to Chinese jurisdiction.[7] The government was anxious to maintain friendly relations with the Powers, whom it saw as needed sources of assistance to the Chinese development effort, and was itself not stable enough to risk challenging the foreigners' position in China. Caught between competing domestic and international tensions, the Nationalists continued to negotiate cautiously and slowly, offering most-favored-nation status to those countries that negotiated treaty revisions. This approach in effect gave foreign governments the ultimate power to determine when and how their special rights in China would end.

Increasing popular vigilance over the unequal treaties issue was not lost on foreign governments, however, which by the mid-1920s began to realize that the days of extraterritoriality in China were numbered and that they could best protect their interests by giving up some rights and territories in order to guarantee a stable, receptive environment for the exploitation of China's "Open Door." By the end of 1928, twenty new treaties had been signed which ended or modified foreigners' special privileges, and China had regained its tariff autonomy.[8] Belgium, France, Denmark, Portugal and Spain relinquished their extraterritorial rights in 1930, subject to the condition that other powers would do the same. Norway and the Netherlands concluded similar agreements a year later. Japan, Sweden, Peru, Brazil and Mexico also exchanged notes with the Nationalist government during this period, reaching agreement on a variety of extraterritoriality issues.[9]

The British, too, began the long process of reducing their presence in China. They renounced their concessions at Hankou and Jinjiang in 1928, and in 1930 they returned the leased territory of Weihaiwei, as promised years before. The British government also began intensive negotiations over extraterritorial rights with the Nationalist government, accepting the principles set forth in the Mandate of December 1929 and agreeing to a gradual abolition of extraterritorial rights. Hong Kong, however, was barely mentioned at these talks, except during discussions on a Chinese nationality law for residents of the colony.[10] From the Nationalists' perspective, extraterritoriality presented a far more pressing burden than did British occupation of Hong Kong. The British, for their part, were adamant about retaining the colony, New Territories included. If the island of Hong Kong had been considered worthless by the British Foreign Office when it was first acquired, by the 1920s the colony played an important role in Great Britain's trade in the Far East. Particularly as the Nanjing government appeared to be taking a more aggressive stance toward foreigners' rights on the mainland, Hong Kong's value as a strictly British outpost increased. Lest anyone doubt Great Britain's resolve in this regard, Governor Clementi in March 1927 made the British position clear: "His Majesty's Government . . . have no intention of surrendering Hong Kong or of abandoning or diminishing in any way its rights or authority in any part of the adjacent mainland territories under British Administration, to the maintenance of which His Majesty's Government attaches the highest importance."[11]

By June 1931 a draft Sino-British treaty on the termination of extraterritorial rights had been drawn up and tentatively agreed to. The Japanese invasion of Manchuria in September, however, forced the Nationalist government to turn its attention to more immediate concerns. In December, the Chinese government postponed the effective date of new jurisdiction regulations and halted bilateral talks. Negotiations would not begin again for a decade.

The Nationalists' Stand on Hong Kong: Chongqing

The Nationalists' diplomatic efforts to renegotiate unequal treaties were suspended between 1931 and 1942 while the government attempted to fight the Japanese threat. The war took an obvious toll on the Nationalists' capacity to rule. It also helped weaken the extraterritoriality system which, as Japanese control spread over a war-ravaged country, ceased to provide benefits to foreign governments.[12] Japanese forces occupied Hong Kong in December 1941, interning its non-Chinese residents and controlling the colony until the war ended in 1945. Though the British commitment to retain Hong Kong never waned, it was during this period that the colony's status for the first time was challenged seriously.

In July 1940, British Prime Minister Winston Churchill and Acting U.S. Secretary of State Sumner Welles publicly declared their governments' intentions to end extraterritoriality when the war was over. Churchill promised "the revision of treaties on a basis of reciprocity and equality."[13] But following the Japanese attack on Pearl Harbor on December 7, 1941, Britain, the U.S. and China became allies against Japan, and plans for treaty revision were accelerated. The British and Americans became anxious to reach an agreement on extraterritoriality with the Chinese, in part as a sign of good faith to an ally (the Americans had long argued that extraterritoriality should be ended anyway), but also to boost the KMT's national prestige and to "keep China in the war."[14]

On U.S. initiative, the British and American governments informed the Chinese formally on October 9, 1942, of their desire to begin negotiations. This allowed the Chinese to publicize the announcement on October 10, the Republic's national day.[15] Negotiations began immediately at the government's wartime headquarters in Chongqing (Chungking). The process was smoother than it had been a decade earlier, since much of the groundwork had already been laid and because the British and Americans were now more inclined to accommodate Chinese demands. By early December, the Americans had in hand the makings of an agreement to end U.S. extraterritorial rights and privileges. The British, however, had reached an impasse with the Chinese over the question of Hong Kong's inclusion in the treaty.

The British negotiating team at Chongqing had fully expected the Chinese to raise the question of the New Territories lease. Chinese interest in terminating the lease had long been recognized, and in May 1942, after learning of British plans to enter into negotiations, the Chinese government proposed publicly that the New Territories lease be terminated. On August 29, 1942, the 100th anniversary of the signing of the Treaty of Nanjing, the Chinese government made a public plea for the abolition of all unequal treaties. A resolution passed by the People's Political Council in November echoed this appeal, calling on the government to "secure in the pending negotiations abrogation of all rights and privileges enjoyed by foreigners in China which contravene the principle of equality."[16]

The Chinese argument for recovery of the New Territories in the 1942 talks was based on the same principles of equality and sovereignty in international law as in the past. Whereas the focus of the negotiations, according to the Americans and British, was to be extraterritorial rights, the Chinese government insisted that its position of international equality, now strengthened by its status as an ally in the war, meant that all unequal treaties should be considered for abrogation.

As in the past, conspicuous by its absence in these negotiations was a specific demand for the return of Hong Kong Island and Kowloon. The treaties under which they were obtained were clearly considered no less "unequal" than the 1898 Convention of Beijing, and their omission can only have been calculated. The Chinese most likely knew, as did the British, that if the New Territories was returned, the rest of the colony would follow. As early as 1928, a British Foreign Office conference had determined that the colony could not survive except as a single entity.[17] A member of the British negotiating team at Chongqing noted that the New Territories was "an essential part of the territory of Hong Kong." He wrote, "The Chinese are probably well aware of these considerations, and by raising the point now are staking their claim for the ultimate rendition of the Colony as a whole to their sovereignty."[18]

From a negotiating standpoint, this made sense. The issue of recovering ceded territories was legally more complex than the question of leaseholds, and the Chinese might have feared it would sidetrack the talks. Having ceded Hong Kong Island and Kowloon "in perpetuity" to Great Britain, the Chinese were hard-pressed to argue, as they could in the case of leaseholds, that they retained sovereignty over the territories. Under the circumstances, they could recover the ceded territories only if they could convince the British that all the treaties considered "unequal" by the Chinese were therefore invalid also, an approach that was unlikely to succeed. Chinese negotiators thus conceded that Hong Kong and Kowloon were "different matters" to be "dealt with separately,"[19] and demanded instead the return of the leased New Territories, for which there was a precedent. Once the Chinese government had recovered the New Territories, it could press its claim for the remainder of the colony through diplomatic channels or, as a possible last resort, squeeze the tiny remaining colony through strikes and trade embargoes until the British yielded.

Chinese negotiators stood firm on this issue. Throughout the talks they pushed for the rendition of the New Territories, while the British, genuinely anxious over the colony's future for perhaps the first time, insisted that it was beyond the scope of the negotiations. As a fall-back position, the Chinese insisted that Great Britain at least should make a statement of intent, either in the treaty itself or in a separate declaration, to return the leased territory. They refused to accept any solution that did not include such a statement.[20]

In their talks with the British, Chinese negotiators referred repeatedly to the strong domestic pressure they faced for the abrogation of unequal treaties. Wellington Koo, the Chinese ambassador to Great Britain who had returned to Chongqing for the talks, attempted to explain to the British the significance of popular opposition to leased territories. He told the British team that he regretted having to take a hard line stance, but, as the British side recorded it, "both the government and Party were committed and could not draw back."[21]

The talks thus moved to the end of December 1942 locked in a stalemate. Tension mounted during the last few days of December as the Americans reported success in their own bilateral talks and indicated they would be ready to sign a treaty with the Chinese on January 1. Determined that their accord be signed simultaneously with the Americans', the British quickly gave in on all the other outstanding issues in the negotiations, even offering a compromise pledge to reconsider the terms of the New Territories lease at a later date.[22] But the Chinese remained unsatisfied with anything less than a declaration of intent to return the territory. The British were determined not to make one, even at the expense of scrapping the treaty altogether.[23]

It looked as if the British would miss their self-imposed deadline when on December 31, the Chinese suddenly and surprisingly acquiesced to the British position, agreeing to reserve the Hong Kong question for a later date. After some time for the preparation of papers, both the British and American treaties were signed on January 11, 1943. In a note to the British ambassador in China on that day, Chinese Foreign Minister Soong wrote, "[whereas] the Chinese Government recognizes that [the] question of [the] lease of [the] New Territories under the Convention of June 9, 1898, is not related to matters under negotiation with the Treaty signed today, it is their desire to raise the question at a more appropriate time." The British agreed that the issue should be raised again "when victory is won."[24]

The reasons for the sudden Chinese capitulation are unclear. It appears likely, however, that the decision was influenced by Wellington Koo, who as an experienced diplomat familiar with British attitudes, counselled Chiang and other officials to postpone discussion of the New Territories.[25] The Chinese government had not abandoned the pursuit, however. In his note, Foreign Minister Soong said he was "sorry" the British were unwilling to discuss the lease:

> The early termination of the Treaty . . . is one of the long-cherished desires of the Chinese people and if effected on the present occasion would go far in the opinion of the Chinese Government to emphasize the spirit of [the] new era which [the] treaty concluded today is intended to inaugurate in [the] relations of [our] two countries. For this reason, I wish to inform you that the Chinese Government reserves its right to propose it again for discussion at a later date.[26]

Chiang Kai-shek's reaction to the outcome of the negotiations, he later wrote, was disappointment. He had reason to hope for a successful resolution of the Hong Kong dispute, particularly since U.S. President Roosevelt strongly supported Chinese territorial claims. The return of Hong Kong, or even a promise to return it, would also have represented a major foreign policy success for Chiang. Under the circumstances, he could only express his determination to regain Hong Kong—this time, the entire colony—at a later date, and reserve what was, at least in principle, the unilateral Chinese right to do so:

> The question of the Kowloon leased territory . . . has been left unsettled in the new treaty with Great Britain. This leaves something to be desired in the cordial relations between China and Great Britain. Hence, on the

(face-saving solution)

day when the Sino-British treaty was signed, the Chinese government formally notified the British government that it was reserving its right to recover Kowloon. The question of the Kowloon leased territory may therefore be raised by the Chinese government at any time. Moreover, our people should realize that Kowloon and Hong Kong are geographically interdependent and their status must be settled simultaneously.[27]

This approach to Hong Kong's status was to become the central formula for justifying the continued presence of a British colony on Chinese soil. At the time, it represented a face-saving solution to a difficult diplomatic problem. The Nationalist government was unwilling to force the issue of Hong Kong's status against obstinate British opposition. For domestic political reasons, however, neither could the KMT allow itself to be perceived as acquiescing to the imperialists. Its compromise position was to maintain a hard line in principle while postponing the ultimate resolution of the colony's status until an "appropriate time," which was intentionally left vague.

Despite Britain's success in keeping Hong Kong out of the Chongqing agreement, President Roosevelt remained hopeful that the colony would be returned. When British Foreign Secretary Sir Anthony Eden visited the United States in March 1943 to discuss postwar arrangements, Roosevelt told T. V. Soong, the Chinese representative in the U.S., that he would propose to Eden a plan for Hong Kong's return. His idea was that Great Britain would take the initiative to return Hong Kong to China, and China would simultaneously declare the territory a free port, promising to protect British interests and residents there.[28]

Roosevelt's proposal was accepted by Chiang Kai-shek, who submitted it to the Supreme National Defense Council. The Council voted to accept the proposal on the condition that China would declare Hong Kong a free port on its own initiative after Great Britain had returned the colony, rather than as an *a priori* condition for its rendition. Soong informed Roosevelt of this decision, but apparently due to a lack of enthusiasm on the British side, no agreement was reached.[29] In fact, it is unlikely the British would have found this proposal persuasive, in light of their adamant desire to maintain administrative control over the colony.

A Second Chance: Hong Kong and the Surrender

Publicly the Chinese were silent about Hong Kong after signing the Chongqing agreement. During a visit to London in July 1943, T. V. Soong did not even raise the issue.[30] The British had promised to reconsider the question when the war was over, and the Chinese apparently took them at their word.

The opportunity to discuss Hong Kong never came, however. And while the war's end brought a new dispute concerning the colony, it took a far different form than at Chongqing. The dispute concerned formal acceptance of the Japanese surrender in Hong Kong and did not deal explicitly with the question of sovereignty, though both the British and Chinese governments clearly appreciated the implicit relationship between the two.[31] The Japanese conceded defeat on August 14, 1945, but in the sixteen days it took Rear-Admiral Sir Cecil Harcourt to arrive with his fleet in Hong Kong's harbor, an intense battle took place over the right to accept the surrender.

Two days after Japan conceded defeat, the Chinese government in Chongqing announced that it was prepared to accept the official surrender in Hong Kong. On August 18, Chiang Kai-shek appealed to U.S. President Truman for his support of the Chinese right to do so.[32] The British government objected, arguing that British sovereignty over the territory gave Great Britain the right to accept the surrender. Truman, who had succeeded Roosevelt upon his death in April 1945, was more sympathetic to the British position in Hong Kong than his predecessor, and he refused to support Chiang. The Generalissimo was insistent, however. He urged that the Japanese surrender be made to his personal representative, with American and British representatives present at the ceremony. After the surrender was complete, he would authorize British troops to reoccupy the territory.[33]

When Truman found that scheme unacceptable as well, Chiang compromised again by offering to delegate his authority to a British commander, who would then accept the Japanese surrender on Chiang's behalf. Truman considered this last suggestion a good one, but it was still unacceptable to the British, who were determined to stand firm on any matter related to their sovereignty in Hong Kong. Left with no choice, Chiang capitulated, agreeing to the British proposal that Rear-Admiral Harcourt accept the surrender on behalf of both Great Britain and Chiang, as supreme commander of the war's China theatre.[34] Chinese troops were present at the surrender, though no attempt was made then or during the British reoccupation of Hong Kong to interfere with British plans.

Chiang had some reason to think that he might be permitted to accept the surrender. Considering China's status as an "equal" ally in the war and its heightened national autonomy after the Chongqing treaties, Chiang may have expected that the British would finally yield some ground on the Hong Kong issue. Similarly, his appeals to Truman reflect the support the Americans had provided in the past on the Hong Kong issue. It seems likely that Chiang's insistence on accepting the Japanese surrender was not an attempt to retrieve the colony, however.

Rather, he apparently saw it as an opportunity to stake a claim to Chinese sovereignty over the territory—a claim that was a central element of the Chinese argument against unequal treaties and one that could have proven useful in future negotiations over Hong Kong.

Having lost the diplomatic battle over the surrender, however, Chiang on August 16 announced that the Chinese had "no territorial ambitions" in the colony,[35] and on August 24 gave a speech that was laced with moderation:

> We will not take advantage of this opportunity to dispatch troops to take over Hong Kong nor will we provoke misunderstanding among our allies. I wish to state here that the present status is regulated by a treaty signed by China and Great Britain. Changes in the future will be introduced only through friendly negotiations between the two countries. Our foreign policy is to honor treaties, rely upon law and seek rational readjustments when the requirements of time and actual conditions demand such readjustments. Now that all the leased territories and settlements in China have been one after another returned to China, the leased territory of Kowloon should not remain an exception, but China will settle this last issue through diplomatic talks between the two countries.[36]

Chiang's expectation that Great Britain soon would agree to negotiations over Hong Kong's return may have led him to moderate his tone. Nevertheless, this statement is remarkable in its willingness to accept the status quo, even granting legitimacy to the so-called "unequal treaties" until the British were willing to reach a diplomatic settlement. Chiang thus continued the pattern, begun at the Washington Conference and reiterated at Chongqing, of postponing resolution of the Hong Kong question. That pattern was to continue for decades.

Relations with the Colony

Relations between Hong Kong and the mainland under the Nationalists, except for a few minor points of friction, were cordial. Customs regulations and the Kowloon-Canton Railway continued to be major topics of bilateral discussion. New agreements were reached regarding arms traffic, telegraph service, aviation, shipping and loans.[37] In 1948, with the Civil War raging, an accord was reached on customs and smuggling that increased Chinese rights in Hong Kong's harbor.[38] In the same year, representatives of the Chinese and Hong Kong governments met to replace boundary markings at the border town of Shataukok.[39]

This period was also marked by several visits to Canton by Hong Kong governors. The first, in 1936, included a meeting with Chiang

Kai-shek, and was followed by a goodwill visit by the Royal Air Force's Singapore Flying Boat.[40] The second took place in 1938. In 1947 Governor Mark Young visited Canton to honor General Chang Fa-kwei, Chiang's personal representative in Canton, for services rendered to Britain during the war. His successor, Sir Alexander Grantham, visited twice later in the same year. General Chang visited Hong Kong twice after the war, in 1946 and 1947, and Guangdong's governor paid an official visit in November 1947, helping to cement the close ties between the two neighboring territories.[41]

There was friction, however, both in Hong Kong's internal politics and in its relations with China. One potential source of dispute arose in 1946, when a massive campaign in Canton attempted to resurrect the 1925–1926 general strike. Some small-scale demonstrations were organized in Hong Kong, but the movement gained little support there and died quickly.[42] Two other incidents involving the Walled City of Kowloon, however, developed into more serious disagreements that forced the Nanjing government to become involved.

The Walled City and the Public Park

The legal status of Kowloon's Walled City, an eleven-acre, densely populated area on the Kowloon Peninsula that was originally known as "Kowloon City," has always been an unsettled element of British administration in Hong Kong. On the insistence of Chinese negotiators, the 1898 Convention of Beijing reserved the city as a special entity in which Chinese administration would continue and Chinese, not British, laws would apply. A British Order in Council of December 1899 amended the treaty to effect the complete incorporation of the Walled City into the colony. The Chinese never recognized that unilateral revision, however, and while never able to exercise authority themselves, later consistently opposed the British claim to jurisdiction there. Through the years, the Walled City developed into a world of its own, crowded, poverty-ridden, a haven for drug users, unlicensed doctors and criminal activity of all kinds.

The first major test to the British claim to jurisdiction occurred in 1933, when the Hong Kong government decided to rid the colony of its public eyesore by levelling the Walled City and building a public park in its place. The first phase of the plan required relocating some residents, and in June 1933 the colonial government informed them that their land was to be taken and compensation provided. The residents, most of whom for personal and professional reasons wished to remain in the Walled City, responded by appealing to the Chinese central and Guangdong provincial governments, which immediately protested to

British authorities. But the Hong Kong government was determined to carry out its gradual relocation program. It proceeded with its plans in spite of Chinese objections, and by the end of the decade had almost completed the demolition. The park, however, was never built, and the Walled City was reoccupied by squatters after World War II.[43]

The Chinese government's argument against eviction, expressed in a series of notes and telegrams to the Hong Kong government between 1933 and 1937, attempted to stake a claim to responsibility for the Walled City's residents. The notes complained that since the Walled City was the ancestral home of its residents and they did not want to move elsewhere, they should not be forced to do so. In addition, eviction would subject them to "the hardship which attaches to homeless persons." The Hong Kong government was urged to "reconsider the matter in a spirit of equality," and to abandon its plan "so as to tally with the spirit of friendliness."[44]

The Chinese statements also accused the Hong Kong government of taking actions that were "at variance with the spirit of the treaty stipulations." Basing their case on the original 1898 treaty and ignoring British revisions, Chinese officials contended that Walled City residents were "in every respect under the control of the Chinese Government" and "the authority of His Excellency the Governor of Hong Kong cannot of course be exercised within the city."[45]

The Chinese did not press their case, however. No attempt had been made to place Chinese officials in the Walled City or to exercise Chinese jurisdiction since they were evicted in 1899, and the Nationalist government was not willing to take a stand on the issue now. It did send a representative to inspect the city and conduct a resident opinion survey, the results of which were included in formal complaints against the Hong Kong government. But this move, like the rest of the Chinese approach, seems to have been made more in deference to the demands of popular opinion than out of a desire to seek redress from the Hong Kong authorities. When Dr. Philip K. C. Tyau, Canton special delegate for foreign affairs, raised the issue during a visit to Hong Kong in 1936, he explained to the colony's governor that "even the Generalissimo [Chiang Kai-shek] feels it necessary on occasion to bow to current opinion in Canton."[46]

The Walled City, 1947–1948

Hong Kong emerged from World War II as the last real pillar of a fading British imperialism in East Asia. The colony's position was also more vulnerable than in the past. Popular support on the mainland for the recovery of Hong Kong had grown, and the Chinese bargaining position vis-à-vis the British had strengthened. The U.S. ambassador to China in 1947 reported that the recovery of the colony had become an "acute issue."[47] In September 1946, the Shanghai City Council had urged Chiang Kai-shek to begin negotiations to recover the territory, and in 1947 the Chinese Foreign Ministry remained hopeful that an agreement could be reached with Great Britain, reporting to the People's Political Council that a "rational solution on the Hong Kong sovereignty problem was within the bounds of possibility."[48] It was in this atmosphere that the Kowloon Walled City again became the subject of conflict.

With the huge influx of Chinese returning or fleeing to Hong Kong after the war, the Walled City was reoccupied by squatters. Early in 1947, the Hong Kong government again decided to take action against the Walled City's unsanitary and unsafe conditions. It announced plans for the resettlement of the area's entire population, some 25,000 people, with 2000 squatters to be moved in the plan's first phase.[49] On January 5, 1948, these squatters were expelled and their huts destroyed. A week later, however, some returned, and police efforts to remove them led to a riot in which one person was killed and dozens injured.

Popular Chinese reaction to the outbreak of violence was strong in Hong Kong and on the mainland. Protesters decried the use of armed police to bully poor Chinese squatters. In Canton, protests turned into a riot, during which the British Consulate was sacked and burned, as were the offices of two major British firms, Butterfield, Swire and Jardine, Matheson. Students in Shanghai declared a two-day protest strike in support of the squatters. Walled City residents were encouraged to continue their militancy and the Nanjing government lodged an official protest with Great Britain, once again claiming sovereignty over the city.[50] The demonstrators in Canton accused the Chinese government of "diplomatic appeasement" and demanded the recovery of Hong Kong, opposition to British imperialism and the ousting of the "dirty British."[51] The protests lasted only a few days, however, and by the end of January the British prepared to continue the demolition of huts, confident that "there was no question of jurisdiction."[52]

The official Chinese reaction to these events was mild. The Nationalists' formal protest to the British government appears to have been a response to the high level of popular agitation that had been aroused over the issue. Meanwhile, the Nanjing government attempted through other channels to defuse all potential for conflict and return stability to the area. The Canton riots, which were apparently not approved by top government officials, were followed by notes of regret to Britain and a promise to punish the rioters. Foreign Minister Wang Shih-ch'ieh, in protesting the use of armed force by the British, also urged that a compromise be reached. After a meeting of KMT leaders in Nanjing,

[handwritten annotation: Developments in China's demonstrated Affect Policy]

strict orders that the incident should be played down were sent to all government departments. The KMT also ordered Chinese newspapers in the mainland and Hong Kong to treat the issue with care and to restrain their anti-British rhetoric.[53]

Negotiations over the issue of Chinese sovereignty in the Walled City and British damage claims lasted for several months after the incident ended. The Chinese government indicated that it would accept a compromise in which the British would retain jurisdiction over the Walled City if Chinese sovereignty were recognized in form.[54] The British were unwilling to accept such an obvious attempt to carve out a space for Chinese sovereignty in the colony, and the Nationalist government did not pursue the issue further. The Walled City's status thus continued to be a particularly ambiguous aspect of China–Hong Kong relations.

[handwritten annotation: Why was China's position to GB strong]

The Nationalists' Approach
to the Hong Kong Question

The Nationalists' more vigorous approach to the Hong Kong question after 1928 reflected major developments in China's domestic and international circumstances. Popular demands for the abrogation of unequal treaties and the assertion of Chinese sovereignty had grown considerably during the 1920s, bringing pressure on the KMT to at least appear to be resolving the issue. The KMT's position vis-à-vis Great Britain also had been strengthened, due to the establishment of a central government at Nanjing and China's status as an ally in World War II. In addition, the decline of the extraterritoriality regime in China during the late 1920s and 1930s, coupled with Roosevelt's support for Hong Kong's return to China, signalled a decline in imperialism that left Hong Kong an increasingly lonely outpost.

In spite of these new circumstances, however, there were limits beyond which the Nationalists were unwilling or unable to force British acquiescence on the Hong Kong question. If the KMT's words were unequivocal, its actions toward the colony were cautious, indicating that foreign interests in Hong Kong or elsewhere in China would not be harmed. On those occasions when conflict arose with Hong Kong, the Nationalist government was hesitant to oppose the British authorities. This approach is reflected in the new formula used to justify postponing resolution of the Hong Kong question: the Chinese government retained its claim to sovereignty, but insisted that the colony's status ultimately would be resolved only when "time requirements and conditions demand," or, as the Communists later would term a similar approach, "when conditions are ripe."

Constraints on Nationalist Policy

The Nationalist government's Hong Kong policy reflected both its new strength and continuing constraints on its policy options. Despite the impressive military success of Chiang Kai-shek's Northern Expedition in 1926–1927, China's political instability and economic underdevelopment continued to limit the Nationalists' ability to push hard on territorial rights issues. The Anti-Japanese and Civil Wars drained the government's resources and dominated its policy agenda, thereby debilitating its capacity to pursue an aggressive policy regarding Hong Kong. And in light of Britain's expressed desire to retain its colony, only an aggressive policy had any chance of being effective. Under these circumstances, real efforts to recover Hong Kong were limited and came only after other treaties relating to extraterritorial rights had been renegotiated. Hong Kong's status also took a back seat to Chiang's main priority regarding national reunification: eradication of the Communist Party.

The Nationalist government's approach to Hong Kong's status also reflected its desire to be respected as a responsible actor in the international arena. One British Foreign Office official in 1929 reportedly stated that "China was trying quite rightly to impress upon the Powers its fitness to take its place among them as a sovereign state," and he therefore "was convinced that [the] Chinese would not regard treaties as scraps of paper."[55] A member of the British negotiating team at Chongqing also noted the importance China seemed to attach to its position as one of the Big Four and an equal leader of the United Nations.[56] Thus while treaty revision was seen as crucial to China's attainment of national autonomy, the Nationalists were not willing to take any actions that other countries might perceive as rash. When the twin goals of national autonomy and international respect came into conflict, KMT leaders tended to adopt a conservative approach. Chiang Kai-shek stated in October 1942 that, "After we have gained equality of status with other nations, we are to exert ourselves and not fall short of our allies' expectations of us or fail to play worthily the part of a modern and independent nation."[57]

There was an important practical aspect to this approach as well. The KMT was in desperate need of whatever support it could gain against its two greatest enemies, the Japanese and the Communists. The British in Hong Kong were perceived as a potential threat to the Japanese. (Indeed, the Chinese were surprised and disappointed when the Japanese were able to occupy Hong Kong rather easily in 1941.) The British government also contributed to China's national construction efforts by providing loans and aid for rail and highway projects.[58] The KMT leadership was further aware that any imprudent actions toward the

British in Hong Kong, despite Roosevelt's support for Chinese claims to the colony, would not be well received by the Americans, who were the KMT's major source of foreign support.

Chinese official and private statements reflect the value placed on good relations with Great Britain. In response to the 1933 Walled City question, the Chinese Foreign Ministry stressed the importance of Sino-British relations and said that "it would scarcely appear expedient to stir up a treaty dispute" over such a small matter.[59] After the Chongqing treaty with the British was signed, Chiang wrote that "this small bit of territory," which had been such a large roadblock at the negotiations, nevertheless should not be allowed "to mar permanent friendly relations between China and Great Britain."[60] And in a private conversation with the U.S. ambassador in 1948, Nationalist Foreign Minister Wang emphasized the primacy of friendly Sino-British relations in Chinese calculations:

> Dr. Wang said that he felt deeply that Anglo-Chinese friendship was essential in the broader world international picture and he was determined insofar as he was able to prevent [the] question of [the] retrocession of Hong Kong from jeopardizing Anglo-Chinese relations. He could not, of course, prevent [a] clamour for retrocession of Hong Kong but he hoped to keep it within bounds which would not unduly disturb China's relations with Britain.[61]

Like governments before and after, the Nationalists took advantage of the opportunities provided by Hong Kong's status. The colony continued during this period to provide useful contacts with the West and served as an essential overseas trade link, particularly when domestic conditions on the mainland made trade difficult. Still one of the world's principal ports, Hong Kong was also an important point of entry for imported weapons, especially from the United States. In the 1930s, seventy percent of China's war needs passed through the colony.[62] The colony's Chinese community also continued to provide funds to the mainland, and Hong Kong served as a safe refuge for Chinese capital.[63]

Hong Kong's role as a political refuge grew dramatically during this period of upheaval on the mainland. Hundreds of thousands of refugees from the Anti-Japanese and Civil Wars escaped to the colony. (Following the Japanese occupation in December 1941, however, refugee traffic moved in the opposite direction.) Hong Kong also became a home for political dissidents and a base for propaganda organs. Both the Communists and Nationalists had bases in Hong Kong where they could publish with reasonable freedom, recruit support, solicit funds and direct activities across the border. Communist activity in the colony was strictly curtailed after the KMT established its Nanjing government, but was permitted to grow again after 1937.

Thus, while their commitment in principle to recovering the territory was genuine, KMT officials recognized that there were important incentives to continue Hong Kong's status quo. These circumstances created a tension that the Nationalists resolved by accepting, even supporting, Hong Kong's status as a British colony in the short term, while postponing the ultimate battle over Chinese sovereignty until conditions were more favorable to the KMT's position. For the Nationalists, that opportunity never arrived.

Notes

1. Wesley R. Fishel, *The End of Extraterritoriality in China* (N.Y.: Octagon Books, 1974): 145–46.

2. *Foreign Relations of the United States, 1928*, vol. 2 (Washington, D.C.: U.S. Government Printing Office): 413–14.

3. *Foreign Relations*, 1928, vol. 2, 416.

4. William L. Tung, *China and Some Phases of International Law* (London: Oxford University Press, 1940): 33; Fishel, *Extraterritoriality*, 170–72.

5. "Manifesto of the National People's Convention Concerning the Abrogation of Unequal Treaties," *The Chinese Social and Political Science Review*, vol. 15 Supplement (1931–1932): 461–65.

6. *Foreign Relations*, 1929, vol. 2, 576–77.

7. Jerome Alan Cohen, ed., *China's Practice of International Law: Some Case Studies* (Cambridge: Harvard University Press, 1972): 256.

8. G. B. Endacott, *A History of Hong Kong*, 2nd ed. (Hong Kong: Oxford University Press, 1977): 289.

9. Fishel, *Extraterritoriality*, 147–48.

10. William Roger Louis, *British Strategy in the Far East, 1919–1939* (London: Clarendon Press, 1971): 161–62.

11. Peter Wesley-Smith, *Unequal Treaty 1898–1997: China, Great Britain and Hong Kong's New Territories* (Hong Kong: Oxford University Press, 1980): 156–57.

12. Fishel, *Extraterritoriality*, 188–89.

13. Fishel, *Extraterritoriality*, 207.

14. Israel Epstein, *The Unfinished Revolution in China* (Boston: Little Brown and Company, 1972): 342.

15. Fishel, *Extraterritoriality*, 210.

16. "Hong Kong Original Correspondence," *Great Britain Colonial Office Papers*, CO 129/588, pt. 1: 6, 33, 285, 70.

17. *Colonial Office*, CO 129/507, 11.

18. *Colonial Office*, CO 129/588, pt. 1: 30.

19. *Colonial Office*, CO 129/588, pt. 1: 117.

20. *Colonial Office*, CO 129/588, pt. 2: 67.

21. *Colonial Office,* CO 129/588, pt. 1: 67.

22. Lau Kit-Ching Chan, "The Hong Kong Question during the Pacific War (1941–1945)," *The Journal of Imperial and Commonwealth History,* 3, no. 1 (Oct. 1973): 67.

23. *Colonial Office,* CO 129/588, pt. 2: 24–25.

24. *Colonial Office,* CO 129/588, pt. 2: 41.

25. William L. Tung, *V. K. Wellington Koo and China's Wartime Diplomacy* (N.Y.: St. John's University Press, 1977): 53.

26. *Colonial Office,* CO 129/588, pt. 1: 102.

27. Chiang Kai-shek, *China's Destiny,* Wang Chung-hui, trans. (N.Y.: De Capo Press, 1976): 17.

28. Hungdah Chiu, "Comparison of the Nationalist and Communist Views of Unequal Treaties," in Cohen, *China's Practice,* 253–54.

29. Chiu, "Comparison," 253–54.

30. Chan, "Hong Kong Question," 69.

31. The Japanese occupied Hong Kong in December 1941 after a convincing defeat of British defenses. British authorities and foreign residents of Hong Kong were interned in the colony until the end of the war. See G. B. Endacott, *Hong Kong Eclipse,* edited and with additional material by Alan P. Birch (Hong Kong: Oxford University Press, 1978).

32. Alan Birch, "Hong Kong in the Balance—August-September, 1945," Working Paper No. CC16, Contemporary Chinese Studies Programme, University of Hong Kong, 1981.

33. Chan, "Hong Kong Question," 73; Lau Kit-Ching Chan, "The United States and the Question of Hong Kong, 1941–1945," *Journal of the Hong Kong Branch of the Royal Asiatic Society,* vol. 19 (1979): 16.

34. Chan, "The United States," 16. When President Roosevelt sent a representative to attempt to persuade Churchill on the Hong Kong issue, Churchill said the colony would be yielded "over my dead body." Quoted in Tung, *V. K. Wellington Koo,* 61.

35. Chan, "The United States," 15.

36. Chinese Ministry of Information, *The Collected Wartime Messages of Generalissimo Chiang Kai-shek, 1937–1945* (N.Y.: John Day Co., 1946): 718.

37. See *Colonial Office,* CO 129/507 through CO 129/595.

38. Gary Catron, *China and Hong Kong, 1945–1967* (Ph.D. Dissertation, Harvard University, 1971): 60.

39. Endacott, *Hong Kong Eclipse,* 314.

40. *Colonial Office,* CO 129/599, 15-17.

41. Endacott, *Hong Kong Eclipse,* 313–14.

42. Catron, *China and Hong Kong,* 49.

43. Wesley-Smith, *Unequal Treaty,* 124–27.

44. *Colonial Office,* CO 129/556, 14; CO 129/546, 40; CO 129/556, 38.

45. *Colonial Office,* CO 129/546, 39.

46. *Colonial Office,* CO 129/556, 30.

47. *Foreign Relations,* 1947, vol. 8: 55.

48. Evan Luard, *Britain and China* (London: Chatto and Windus, 1962): 182.

49. Catron, *China and Hong Kong*, 54; Wesley-Smith, *Unequal Treaty*, 127.

50. Catron, *China and Hong Kong*, 55-57; Wesley-Smith, *Unequal Treaty*, 127.

51. *Foreign Relations*, 1948, vol. 8: 49.

52. *Foreign Relations*, 1948, vol. 8: 63.

53. Catron, *China and Hong Kong*, 56–58; *Foreign Relations*, 1948, vol. 8: 66-67.

54. Catron, *China and Hong Kong*, 58.

55. *Foreign Relations*, 1929, vol. 2: 628.

56. *Colonial Office*, CO 129/588, pt. 1: 160.

57. Chinese Ministry of Information, *Wartime Messages*, 717–18.

58. Irving S. Friedman, *British Relations with China, 1931–1939* (N.Y.: Institute of Pacific Relations, 1940): 226; Chan, "Hong Kong Question," 58.

59. *Colonial Office*, CO 129/544, 29.

60. Chiang, *China's Destiny*, 143.

61. *Foreign Relations*, 1948, vol. 8: 68.

62. Jan Morris, *Hong Kong* (N.Y.: Random House, 1988): 300.

63. *Foreign Relations*, 1947, vol. 8: 715.

4

The People's Republic: Anti-Imperialism and British Colonialism

The Communist victory and subsequent establishment of the People's Republic of China in 1949 brought to the country a new political era with immediate and significant implications for Hong Kong. Unlike the Nationalists, the Communists were able to establish a strong central government that ruled a largely unified China. The CCP came to power through an impressive military victory and its new regime was saddled with fewer obligations to foreign powers than the KMT had been. The Communist government therefore was in a far more advantageous position than its predecessors to seek a resolution to Hong Kong's status.

This capability was buttressed by the CCP's well-known and virulent opposition to imperialism and colonialism. Like the KMT, the CCP had long favored the abrogation of unequal treaties, but where the Nationalists favored a gradual process that involved negotiating new treaties, the Communist position was far more radical. From the CCP's perspective, the unequal treaties were vestiges of a brutal foreign imperialism that the Chinese were obliged to destroy if they were to achieve the national autonomy that was a central goal of the revolution. Under these circumstances, the colony's position might have seemed precarious. A product of unequal treaties and a blatant monument to British colonialism, Hong Kong represented much that the Chinese revolution claimed to oppose. Yet alongside the PRC, Hong Kong not only continued to survive as a British colony, but flourished.

The Chinese Communist Party and Hong Kong Before 1949

Leading members of the Chinese Communist Party were familiar with the Hong Kong question long before 1949. In the 1920s, the CCP had already marked Hong Kong, as the product of unequal treaties, for return to the mainland. The CCP took part in labor organization in the colony, and Party members played an influential role in the 1925–1926 Strike-Boycott. After the KMT's split with the CCP in 1927, however, Hong Kong authorities moved to eliminate Communist organizations and propaganda in the colony, a policy that lasted until the start of the second KMT-CCP United Front in 1937.

During the Civil War, Hong Kong became a valuable outpost for the Communists. Sheltered from Nationalist forces and allowed by British authorities to operate, the CCP was able to solicit support, direct activities on the mainland, make overseas contacts, publish propaganda, harbor exiles and assure the safe passage of troops to "liberated" areas. Zhou Enlai relied heavily on communications outlets in Hong Kong to conduct the CCP's foreign affairs in the late 1940s.[1] Hong Kong was also used as a base for smuggling arms and for conducting intelligence work in Guangdong.[2] The Party's 5000 members in Hong Kong between 1946 and 1949 included a host of intellectuals and writers who would have found it impossible to work on the mainland. Even after 1948, when CCP membership became illegal in Hong Kong, the Party carried on in secret while British authorities turned a blind eye.

In part because it feared losing its freedom to operate in Hong Kong, the Communist Party apparatus acted cautiously there. Despite the Party's opposition to colonialism, Party journals usually praised rather than condemned the Hong Kong government. Even when the British cracked down on Communist activities in the spring and summer of 1949, outlawing politically-oriented strikes, closing some schools and taking action against a Communist newspaper, complaints were kept within strict bounds. The CCP's news organ, the New China News Agency (NCNA), called Hong Kong a "city of terror" and accused British authorities of complicity with American imperialists. But the CCP refrained from stirring up protest in the colony. The leftist *Wen Wei Po* assured readers that Hong Kong's colonial status would not be challenged, and the Communist *Hua Shang Pao* emphasized that Hong Kong was not a target of the revolution on the mainland.[3]

The CCP's Official Position on Hong Kong

The Communist Party's formal stand against imperialism and colonialism was explicitly stronger than the KMT's. In essays and speeches, Chairman Mao Zedong criticized the KMT for collaborating with the forces of imperialism. His 1939 essay, "The Chinese Revolution and the Chinese Communist Party," referred specifically to unequal treaties, the British seizure of Hong Kong and the "ruthless rule" of imperialists who tried to "poison the minds of the Chinese people." The Communist Party, Mao argued, was leading the struggle against the foreign powers. The Party's goals were decidedly antiforeign, its "primary and foremost task being the national revolution to overthrow imperialism," particularly British and American imperialism.[4]

The CCP also did not couch its anti-imperialist rhetoric in conciliatory language designed to calm the fears of foreign governments. Whereas Chiang Kai-shek insisted that China would continue to rely on the support of "friendly" Western countries, Mao Zedong was less sanguine about the prospect of gaining real assistance from erstwhile oppressors. "'We need help from the British and U.S. governments.' This, too, is a naive idea in these times. Would the present rulers of Britain and the United States, who are imperialists, help a people's state? . . . Throughout his life, Sun Yat-sen appealed countless times to the capitalist countries for help and got nothing but heartless rebuffs."[5]

The CCP's foreign policy was to be based on three principles: equality, mutual benefit and mutual respect for territorial sovereignty and integrity. The Common Program, an interim Chinese constitution adopted by the Chinese People's Political Consultative Conference (CPPCC) in September 1949, reiterated these principles and stressed the incompatibility of imperialism with the new Chinese government.[6] The Common Program's position on treaties signed previously with foreign governments was more cautious, however, promising to "recognize, abrogate, revise or renegotiate them according to their respective contents."[7]

As for Hong Kong, the CCP's position was more clear in principle than in practice. The agreements that handed Hong Kong to Great Britain were considered unequal treaties that would have to be abrogated. The Communists' interest in resolving the Hong Kong question was revealed during the Amethyst Affair of 1949, when the Chinese seized a British gunboat travelling on the Yangtze River. In a private meeting in May 1949 with a representative of the American ambassador in China, a top Communist official demanded that the British agree to discuss the Hong Kong question as part of a proposed settlement of the dispute.[8] That demand was made moot, however, after the Amethyst escaped on its own, a turn of events the Communists probably welcomed. After the incident, the CCP made no public demands for negotiations with the British over Hong Kong nor took any steps that might stir conflict within the colony or between the colony and the mainland. Trade with Hong Kong continued unabated.

Ardent opposition to imperialism and principled advocacy of equality, sovereignty and territorial integrity continued to be mainstays of Chinese foreign policy after 1949. While these principles were repeated often, however, their meaning in real terms and their specific relevance to the

Hong Kong question were vague. For all the CCP's opposition to unequal treaties, for example, one is hard pressed to find a definition of the term in Chinese texts. An international trade textbook published in 1958 offers perhaps the clearest indication of how the Communists understood the concept:

> The classical writers of Marxism-Leninism confirmed an important principle concerning international treaties, namely that genuine equality between all parties should become the foundation of international treaties. Lenin said: 'Negotiations can only be conducted between equals and, therefore, genuine equality between both sides is an essential condition for reaching a genuine agreement.'
>
> Consequently, in accordance with Marxism-Leninism, there are equal and unequal treaties, and therefore, progressive mankind takes fundamentally different attitudes towards different kinds of treaties. Equal treaties should be strictly obeyed. Unequal treaties are in violation of international law and without legal validity.[9]

In the same year, a group of legal scholars published a critique of the "old law viewpoint" in international legal studies that argued, "Equal treaties are treaties concluded on the basis of equality between the parties; unequal treaties are those which do not fulfill this elementary requirement . . . [and they] are not legally binding." The article continued, "In order to rectify the unjust situation created by history, a state must recover sovereignty over its own territory. This is confirmed by the practice of modern international law."[10]

There never was any doubt about Hong Kong's inclusion among the territories whose sovereignty would have to be recovered. The CCP had always included the colony in its remonstrations against imperialism in China. An article on state territory and international law published in 1960 referred specifically to the lease of the New Territories, which it called a form of "derivative acquisition" under bourgeois international law.

> Like cession, it is a method by which imperialist countries seek to seize territory from weak and small countries. [Leases of Chinese territory by the Powers] were acquired by concluding unequal treaties. These unequal treaties absolutely were not concluded through 'peaceful negotiations' . . . as a matter of fact, lease of the above-mentioned [Jiaozhou] Bay and other places was executed under threat of force. . . . The leases of Wei-hai-wei and Kowloon were also obtained under similar conditions.[11]

The article compared Britain's lease of Chinese territory to the "imperialist" Americans' acquisition of military bases around the world.

"There is no difference in the method they employed. Both bases and territory were obtained by means of concluding unequal treaties."[12]

Nevertheless, the PRC had no clear policy regarding the resolution of Hong Kong's status, nor was there any indication that Party and government policy makers devoted substantial attention to the issue. When challenged, Chinese officials responded by restating well-known principles concerning Hong Kong's status but avoided any hint of likely confrontation over the issue. In early 1963, for example, the Communist Party of the United States criticized the PRC for acquiescing to British imperialism by allowing Hong Kong to remain in British hands. In March, a sharply-worded editorial in *People's Daily* responded, explaining that Hong Kong's colonial status was created by nineteenth-century imperialists who forced Qing officials to sign unequal treaties. The editorial insisted on the PRC's unilateral right to resolve the Hong Kong question but indicated that it would maintain a conservative approach toward the colony. In further defense of Chinese policy, the editorial argued that allowing the British to remain in Hong Kong should not be interpreted as compromising China's territorial integrity:

> At the time the People's Republic of China was inaugurated our government declared that it would examine the treaties concluded by previous Chinese governments with foreign governments, treaties that had been left over from history, and would recognize, abrogate, revise or renegotiate them according to their respective contents. . . . With regard to the outstanding issues, which are a legacy from the past, we have always held that, when conditions are ripe, they should be settled peacefully through negotiations and that, pending a settlement, the *status quo* should be maintained. Within this category are the questions of Hong Kong, Kowloon and Macau.
>
> Anyone with a discerning eye can see at once that your sole intention is to prove that the Chinese are cowards. To be frank, there is no need for the Chinese people to prove their courage and staunchness in combatting imperialism by making a show of force on the questions of Hong Kong and Macau."[13]

During a visit to London one month later, Chinese Vice-Minister of Foreign Trade Lu Xuzhang reassured British officials again that the PRC did not intend to reclaim Hong Kong in the near future.[14]

As Sino-Soviet relations worsened in the early 1960s, the Soviets attempted to embarrass the Chinese over Hong Kong. They charged the PRC not only with failing to expel the British from Hong Kong, but with "peacefully collaborating with British and American capital in Hong Kong" and "jointly exploiting the working people."[15] In September 1964, a meeting in Moscow of the World Youth Forum affronted the Chinese deliberately by including Hong Kong and Macau in a resolution on the elimination of colonies in Asia. The PRC was quick to brush off such criticism. In response to the Youth Forum resolution, NCNA accused the Soviet Union of "interfering in the internal affairs of China and encroaching on its sovereignty," and reiterated the PRC's intention to recover Hong Kong and Macau "at an appropriate time."[16]

The Chinese government was pressured again in 1973 to explain its position on Hong Kong and Macau. The United Nations Special Committee on Colonialism had included the two territories on its list of remaining colonies, and U.N. Ambassador Huang Hua presented a letter to the committee explaining why they should be omitted:

> As is known to all, the questions of Hong Kong and Macau belong to the category of questions resulting from the series of unequal treaties left over by history, treaties which the imperialists imposed on China.
>
> Hong Kong and Macau are part of Chinese territory occupied by the British and Portuguese authorities. The settlement of the questions of Hong Kong and Macau is entirely within China's sovereign right and does not at all fall under the ordinary category of colonial territories. . . .
>
> With regard to the questions of Hong Kong and Macau, the Chinese Government has consistently held that they should be settled in an appropriate way when conditions are ripe. The United Nations has no right to discuss these questions.[17]

This and other statements demonstrate that the Communists, like the Nationalists, were insistent that other nations recognize the fundamental principle of Chinese sovereignty over Hong Kong. Unlike the Nationalists, however, the Communists chose not to argue in legal terms, for example by invoking *rebus sic stantibus*. This is probably because any attempt to present such an argument would have amounted to a tacit acceptance of the original validity of the treaties. The CCP's consistent position was that unequal treaties, simply because of the circumstances under which they were signed, were never valid.

While this approach in principle allowed PRC officials to demand the return of Hong Kong at any time, regardless of the 1997 deadline, it also gave them a justification to ignore that deadline and postpone resolution of Hong Kong's status indefinitely. Indeed, official Chinese statements after 1949 made no reference to a planned recovery of Hong Kong. The PRC was extremely reluctant to make public its claims to the colony, no matter how justified they believed them to be. The most specific pronouncements came only when the Chinese felt pressured to respond to events in Hong Kong or to challenges from third parties. As a "question left over from history," the Hong Kong issue was a particularly thorny one, and the Communist government after 1949 preferred to leave it alone.

The government in Beijing did not agree with all aspects of British rule in Hong Kong, however, and on occasion it took the initiative in criticizing the colonial government. During the 1958 Taiwan Straits Crisis and again during the Vietnam War, the PRC accused the British in Hong Kong of colluding with American imperialists and threatened that they would be held responsible for their actions. These criticisms were meant mainly for propaganda purposes, however, and did not challenge directly the British right to rule Hong Kong. And despite the hard-line stance of some Foreign Ministry statements, the Communists avoided taking measures that could harm the colony's stability or imply that the PRC intended to recover it. Rather, the PRC's behavior on the whole reveals considerable patience and a willingness to take advantage of the benefits provided by British-ruled Hong Kong.

PRC policy toward Macau, the Portuguese colony located on the opposite side of the Pearl River estuary from Hong Kong, reflected the same approach. In 1955, in reaction to a festival planned to celebrate the 400th anniversary of the Portuguese occupation, *People's Daily* published a statement that could be considered equally valid for Hong Kong: "Macau is Chinese territory. The Chinese people have never forgotten that they have the right to demand the recovery of this territory from the hands of Portugal. The fact that Macau has not yet been returned to China does not mean that the Chinese people can tolerate long continuation of the occupation of Macau."[18]

As in the case of Hong Kong, however, the PRC was in fact willing to tolerate foreign rule for the foreseeable future. Macau's circumstances were different from Hong Kong's—the territory was not leased, and it did not generate the kinds of economic and other benefits that Hong Kong provided to the mainland—but Chinese officials grouped the colonies together as the last two vestiges of foreign imperialism in China. They also recognized that any attempt to alter Macau's status would send a threatening signal to Hong Kong and cause a crisis there. Thus the Chinese reportedly turned down Portuguese offers in the 1960s and 1970s to return the territory. Over the years, they insisted that Macau's status would be resolved at the same time as Hong Kong's. Indeed, after the Sino-British agreement was signed, the Chinese quickly reached agreement with Portugal to recover Macau in 1999.

Relations with the Colony

Chinese relations with Hong Kong since the Communist revolution have not always been smooth. Several incidents caused friction between

Hong Kong and Beijing, and Hong Kong's colonial status has always been a sore point in Anglo-Chinese relations. The dominant trend in the PRC's relations with the colony, however, has been the establishment of broad-based, friendly ties and *de facto* recognition of British sovereignty. The Communists since 1949 have treated their boundary with Hong Kong as an international border (albeit with special treatment for Chinese travellers) and Chinese merchant vessels have continued to fly the British flag in Hong Kong's harbor. Hong Kong and the PRC have reached numerous commercial and other agreements, some of them central to the colony's growth. Government officials at all levels have met formally, including visits by Hong Kong governors to Beijing, though the Chinese government has usually referred to Hong Kong officials as "British authorities in Hong Kong," to avoid the appearance of legitimizing British sovereignty in the colony.

PRC policy after 1949 reflected an active desire to build relations with the colony rather than a grudging acceptance of the status quo. By 1950, trade with Hong Kong had reached a postwar peak, double the 1948 level.[19] During the Korean War, a United Nations trade embargo against China that Hong Kong was required to honor caused a dramatic drop in China–Hong Kong trade, but after the war trade again grew steadily. In 1964, Hong Kong surpassed the Soviet Union as the top consumer of Chinese goods, and economic ties between Hong Kong and the mainland, including Chinese investment in the colony, continued to expand. Continuing a pattern set decades before, the mainland provided a major share of the colony's food, and Hong Kong provided a considerable portion of China's foreign exchange earnings.[20]

The PRC made a standing offer to supply water to Hong Kong in 1960, and an agreement was signed on November 15 of that year, with the tap turned on in December.[21] One report said that the Chinese were willing to provide water free of charge, as they did to Macau, but Hong Kong authorities insisted on paying. In 1963, an extensive drought in South China put water resources under serious strain, but supplies to Hong Kong continued, albeit in slightly reduced quantities, even though the difficulties involved permitted the Chinese only a small profit.[22]

Increased trade over the years has been accompanied by greater contact in other areas as well. Talks on the resumption of through-passenger train service were conducted without success from 1955 to 1957, but they were resumed in 1959 and reached agreement in late 1960.[23] A series of cultural exchanges began in 1955[24] and blossomed again in the 1970s, as China sent scholars and businessmen to conduct research, make external contacts and learn from the colony's success. Eventually China became directly involved in Hong Kong's financial environment, buying land, investing, participating in construction projects and playing an active role in the banking sector. During the visit of British Foreign Secretary Sir Alec Douglas-Home to China in 1972, the two sides agreed that cooperation in a wide range of fields, including trade, communications, transportation and power, should be developed further. At the same time, Chinese officials reportedly promised that they would not press for Hong Kong's return for an indefinite period.[25]

Nevertheless, there have been tense moments in China–Hong Kong relations since 1949. Several incidents brought to the fore the question of Hong Kong's position as a British colony and the implicit Chinese acceptance of its status quo. Each of these confrontations reveals both sides of Chinese policy: a principled opposition to the usurpation of Chinese sovereignty and a practical willingness to accept circumstances as they exist—indeed, to avoid moves that might appear to challenge the British position in the colony.

At the Border, 1949

The Communist victory in 1949 provided the best opportunity any Chinese leadership had ever had to recover Hong Kong. The People's Liberation Army (PLA), though weary and overextended by the time it reached Canton, nevertheless had just completed a convincing military victory and was riding a wave of unprecedented nationalist sentiment. The foreign "imperialists" and their "running dogs," the KMT forces led by Chiang Kai-shek, were being forced out of China. A military occupation of Hong Kong would have seemed an appropriate step for a new government committed to reestablishing China's territorial integrity. In addition, the rapid British capitulation to Japanese troops in 1941 had shown that the colony was not easily defensible. In a conversation with the U.S. consul general in Beijing in August 1949, a member of the Chinese Democratic League observed that the Communists "were filled with confidence after their 'victory' in Shanghai" and predicted that they would attack Hong Kong immediately after securing Canton.[26]

But British forces, bolstered by reinforcements that had been brought in against the possibility of attack, were never tested. As early as August 1949 it became evident that the Communists did not intend any military moves against the colony. The CCP did not mobilize internal propaganda organs against the Hong Kong or British governments.[27] Qiao Guanhua (also known as Qiao Mu), Communist spokesman in the colony, explained that the Hong Kong question could only be settled at the "highest level," indicating that military actions would be avoided and that a diplomatic approach to the colony would be adopted. And in late September 1949, the director of China's Institute of Social Sciences told the U.S. consul general in Shanghai that Hong Kong's position could be considered safe, since it had been decided in CCP subcommittees that all treaties signed before the Nationalists came to power would, at least for the time being, be honored.[28]

In spite of the fears of Hong Kong residents and the military preparations of the British, the arrival of PLA troops at the Hong Kong border in mid-October 1949 was a quiet affair. Karl S. Rankin, U.S. consul general in the colony, recorded the events:

> While the occupation of Canton passed off as peacefully as could have been expected, developments along the Hong Kong frontier were even more gratifying to the British authorities. Only a handful of Nationalist soldiers sought refuge in the colony, while regular Communist troops apparently did not approach closer than twenty-five miles from the frontier. Communist guerrilla units occupied the Chinese border posts but caused no trouble. . . . At the close of October no regular Communist formations had appeared at the frontier, and all was quiet.[29]

Reports soon reached Hong Kong that Guangdong authorities were anxious to reopen the Kowloon-Canton Railroad as soon as possible. The new government announced that no PLA regulars would be stationed at the frontier and that there would be no interference with trade.[30] PRC officials, like government officials in Hong Kong, were clearly anxious for conditions at the border to return to the status quo ante as quickly as possible.

The 1952 Comfort Mission

Despite Chinese willingness to let Hong Kong continue to function as in the past, peaceful relations were upset on several occasions in the early 1950s by incidents in Hong Kong that drew criticism from the Chinese government. In each case, after stating its position, the Chinese government moved quickly to defuse the conflict.

The incident that created the greatest stir in the early postrevolutionary years began with a fire in late December 1951 that destroyed several thousand squatter shacks. Communist newspapers accused the British of deliberately setting the blaze and refusing to fight it, in order to clear land for extension of the nearby airport.[31] A citizens' group in Canton then announced that it planned to send a "comfort mission" to the colony to deliver money collected in Canton on behalf of the homeless victims. The group also announced plans to gather materials related to political persecution in Hong Kong.[32]

The Hong Kong government announced that it would refuse entry to the comfort mission from Canton, but some 5000 people turned out at the train station to greet it anyway. When they were told that the mission had been denied entrance into the colony, a riot erupted. One person was killed, several were injured and several police cars were burned. Hong Kong authorities later closed the Communist Hong Kong newspaper, *Ta Kung Pao,* and put several editors and publishers on trial for sedition after they published the PRC's version of the incident, which was critical of the Hong Kong government.[33]

Official Chinese reaction to the riot was strong. Beijing accused the British of persecution, particularly by denying political and economic rights to Hong Kong's Chinese residents. *People's Daily* said that British heads would be smashed and *Lianhe Bao* asserted that "Hong Kong will one day be liberated from the savage and despotic rule of the imperialists."[34] A May 1952 Foreign Ministry statement charged that there had been a number of fires of suspicious origin in poverty-stricken areas of the colony, after which the British imperialists had refused to aid victims or allow them to receive outside assistance. For these and other atrocities, the statement concluded, the British government would be held fully responsible.[35] These statements appear to have been intended only for propaganda purposes, however. Their position stated, the Chinese were willing to let tensions dissipate, and their threats had no real effect in Hong Kong.

Immigration, 1956 and 1962

One persistent PRC complaint after 1949 concerned Hong Kong's immigration restrictions. The colony regulated entry from China according to a quota system that the Chinese government considered unreasonable, in part because it denied Chinese citizens free right of travel in an area that was held in principle to be Chinese territory, and in part because it was thought illogical that such limits were necessary, since few Chinese in the PRC would truly desire to leave the motherland and live under British domination. Hong Kong authorities responded to PRC pressure on this issue in February 1956 by dropping the quota system. In the following six months, 56,000 people entered the colony, where most soon became permanent residents. Swamped by the huge number of immigrants and unable to gain Beijing's assistance in slowing the flow, the Hong Kong government reimposed the quotas.[36]

The Chinese government reacted angrily to this unilateral action. Prime Minister Zhou Enlai stated publicly that the British should not interfere with normal international traffic and that Hong Kong residents were being denied their rights. Beijing even threatened to cut off the negotiations on through-passenger train service then in progress. This threat carried little weight, however, since the negotiations were already deadlocked. Furthermore, Zhou's reference to the international border conceded, rather than challenged, British control over the territory. Beijing also rejected the possibility of pressuring the Hong Kong government from within the colony and warned residents there to refrain from causing disruption over the issue. According to *Ta Kung Pao*, it was the duty of Overseas Chinese, as well as Hong Kong and Macau residents, that "while maintaining their own legitimate rights and interests they must not take part in the political strife of the countries of their domicile, but must respect the local customs and law."[37]

A dispute over immigration erupted again in 1962 when, during a severe famine that resulted from China's failed Great Leap Forward, Guangdong officials reportedly encouraged residents to cross the border into Hong Kong. The huge influx of refugees overwhelmed the colony's newly established Immigration Department, which over a six-week period in May and June apprehended and returned to China more than 62,000 illegal immigrants. It was estimated that an equal number evaded authorities and settled in the colony.[38] The refugee flood was halted only after the British chargé d'affaires in Beijing complained directly to Zhou Enlai.

After this incident, the Hong Kong government was again able to limit the influx of immigrants into the colony. But over the years a steady stream of PRC residents, often tens of thousands per year, immigrated to Hong Kong. An even larger number entered illegally and evaded authorities long enough to establish residence. The immigration problem, which has been a constant topic of discussion between Hong Kong and mainland officials, dramatizes the marked differences in lifestyle and standard of living on opposite sides of the border, a gap that began to narrow only in the 1980s. The immigrants themselves are an obvious reminder of the human aspect of the Hong Kong question. The debate over Hong Kong's future concerns not only territory but an entire population. It is not surprising that Hong Kong's Chinese immigrants, particularly those who left illegally, were among those most alarmed by plans to return the colony to the PRC.

The Double-Ten Riots, 1956

On several occasions since 1949, Hong Kong's internal peace has been disrupted by violent rioting. The first riots, in 1956, were set off by a seemingly innocuous event. On the morning of October 10, the anniversary of the 1911 Revolution that is celebrated by the KMT as China's national day, a Chinese manager at one of Kowloon's apartment complexes tore down Nationalist flags that residents had posted on a wall. Though the manager was acting according to building regulations, a crowd gathered and demanded that the flags be allowed to remain. As the situation became tense, police were called in, but the crowd's size grew and violence broke out. Fueled by the involvement of triad gangs, rioting spread through the colony and became increasingly violent. Attacks were mounted on Communist organizations, offices and schools. On the afternoon of October 11, the Hong Kong government called in troops to quell the disturbances and imposed a curfew. The rioting slowed, and by October 12 the curfew was lifted in most places. By the time the incident ended, 59 people were dead and 500 had been injured. Six thousand arrests were made and four executions for murder were later carried out. Property damage totalled nearly one million U.S. dollars.[39]

To officials in Beijing, the rioting appeared to be the work of the KMT in collusion with the British, meant as a slap in the face to the PRC and to Communists in Hong Kong. Suspicions of Britain's anti-PRC intentions had been raised a year earlier, when an airplane carrying a delegation of PRC officials to a major international conference exploded after takeoff from Hong Kong's airport. The bomb's apparent target was Chinese Premier Zhou Enlai, who turned out not to have been on the flight, and the main suspect in the case fled to Taiwan. Beijing roundly criticized the Hong Kong administration for allowing the sabotage to take place.

After the 1956 rioting, the British chargé d'affaires in Beijing was summoned twice to receive criticism from Zhou Enlai and Vice Foreign Minister Zhang Hanfu for damage done to the property of Hong Kong Chinese and the "cold-blooded murders and looting by KMT agents." They blamed British authorities for failing to stop the disturbance and for inadequate protection of Chinese lives and property.[40] A *People's Daily* editorial on October 24, 1956, one of three that criticized the Hong Kong government's handling of the rioting, issued a stern warning:

> The Chinese people will not stand quietly by and disregard the safety of the Chinese who live in Hong Kong and Kowloon. We are not prepared to tolerate the use of Hong Kong and Kowloon as a base for acts of sabotage against China. . . . We demand Hong Kong authorities to immediately change such attitude which we cannot bear, thoroughly to take measures regarding this riotous affair, strictly punish criminal head of KMT agents and indeed to take care of the life and security of the Chinese residents.[41]

Beijing further accused the British of colluding with the KMT under American direction, lying in their official report on the riots and being secretly pleased that Chinese people were injured.[42] Zhou Enlai asserted that the Chinese government reserved the right to make demands of the Hong Kong government in the future, though it was not clear what specific demands, if any, he had in mind.[43] When he met later with Hong Kong Governor Sir Alexander Grantham in Beijing, Zhou reportedly promised that British rule in the colony would not be challenged as long as three conditions were met: (1) Hong Kong did not serve as a military base for foreign anti-Chinese forces, a reference to the U.S. Seventh Fleet, (2) the Hong Kong government prevented subversive acts against the PRC, and (3) Hong Kong authorities guaranteed the safety of Chinese officials working in the colony.[44]

These conditions may have reflected genuine concern among the Chinese leadership that Hong Kong could become a base for anti-PRC intrigue. But the British were already well aware of their vulnerable position in Hong Kong. They were cautious then, as later, to limit activities that might appear threatening to the Communist government. Their restraint in that regard helped facilitate the PRC's accommodation of the colony.

Resettlement, 1957

The Chinese government was again called to the assistance of its Hong Kong "compatriots" in the spring of 1957. The colonial government had decided to move 7000 people from their homes in order to clear land for construction of a resettlement estate near the airport. As in previous cases of resettlement, the Chinese Foreign Ministry complained in a note to the British government that the residents were unwilling to move and were not given adequate compensation. A second note expressed "extreme wrath" at the British attempt to "deny the Chinese government its legitimate rights to protect from infringement the legitimate interests of the Chinese residents of Hong Kong and Kowloon."[45]

The Chinese demanded that fair compensation be paid and that no more forced evictions be carried out.[46] The issue ended there, however. No attempt was made to support internal opposition to the relocation plan, and the Hong Kong government continued with its construction project. The PRC later would restate its claim to responsibility for Hong Kong's Chinese residents, but it never demonstrated any intention to act on that claim.

The Walled City, 1962–1963

In 1962, the Kowloon Walled City again became the focus of controversy. The Hong Kong government in March informed residents in a section of the city that they were to be moved and their premises demolished to make room for a resettlement estate. The residents organized in opposition to the plan and requested Beijing's support.[47] The Chinese central government responded by issuing two formal protests that called the demolition plan "intolerable" and "a grave violation of China's sovereignty."[48] They accused the British of an "utterly truculent and vicious attitude" and reasserted the old claim that, "The [Walled] City of Kowloon is Chinese territory and within China's jurisdiction, and this has been so [all] along in history."[49]

Despite these harsh words, however, Chinese officials were apparently anxious to settle the matter quickly and quietly. Before taking a public stance, the Chinese Foreign Ministry summoned the British chargé in Beijing and urged Hong Kong authorities to reconsider the relocation plans. Only a week later, after the Hong Kong government announced a detailed demolition schedule, did the Chinese lodge their formal protests.[50] However, it appears they did not back up their protest by providing material support for a local opposition group in Hong Kong. In the end, the issue was resolved by capitulation on the part of the Hong Kong government which, apparently in deference to the strong opposition sentiment, deferred its demolition plans.

The Cultural Revolution and Hong Kong, 1967

These points of friction between the PRC and Hong Kong were minor blips in a relationship that in general was cooperative and peaceful. That peace was shattered in 1967, however, by seven months of rioting and disorder associated with the Cultural Revolution in the mainland.[51] The riots left 51 people dead and 800 injured. Five thousand people were arrested for violence that cost the colony millions of dollars in property and economic damage.[52]

China's Great Proletarian Cultural Revolution got under way in the late spring of 1966, and in August throngs of Maoist "Red Guards" marched in Beijing, initiating its most radical phase. In December, riots flared in Macau, severely damaging the authority of the Portuguese administration there. Hong Kong government officials and leftists in Hong Kong paid close attention to these events, but there were no clear indications from Beijing that Hong Kong was to be a target of the movement.

During the first few months of 1967, Hong Kong experienced an influx of Maoist propaganda and an increase in labor disputes. Workers at one company in Kowloon that manufactured artificial flowers went on strike to protest harsh new rules concerning shift length and working conditions. Their demands were typical enough, but the dispute escalated when the company dismissed 97 workers and closed two plants. In early May, several thousand people demonstrated against police treatment of the striking workers, and the Hong Kong government responded by activating riot police.[53]

Hong Kong leftists seized this opportunity to turn labor demands into political demands and began to call publicly for an end to British oppression. Inspired by developments across the border, they organized the Committee of Hong Kong–Kowloon Chinese Compatriots of all Circles for the Struggle Against Persecution by the British Authorities in Hong Kong and staged demonstrations, including a march on the governor's mansion. The "Struggle Committee" also organized work stoppages and strikes in a number of industries, most notably transportation, that reportedly involved 60,000 workers.[54] Beginning in July, the leftist movement escalated further, including a violent bombing campaign.

There was some support for the movement among radicals in the Chinese leadership. Through its All-China Federation of Trade Unions, the PRC supplied US$3.3 million to the Struggle Committee. Massive rallies were held in Canton to demonstrate support for the movement in Hong Kong. Sino-British relations reached a low point, as Beijing ordered a British diplomat out of the country in May and in August announced that no personnel of the British chargé's office could leave China without permission. Rallies were held in major Chinese cities to show support for the anti-British struggle, and in Shanghai Red Guards ransacked the British Consulate. In retaliation for the arrest in Hong Kong of several left-wing journalists, Chinese authorities placed Reuters Correspondent Anthony Grey under house arrest in Beijing, where he remained for two years. Even food shipments to the colony were stopped for four days, causing a serious food shortage, and PRC officials refused Hong Kong's request for an increase in the supply of water to the colony.[55]

The British chargé d'affaires was summoned to the Chinese Foreign Ministry on several occasions to listen to some of the most vitriolic criticisms ever made against the British presence in Hong Kong. Editorials in *People's Daily* and statements by Chinese officials accused the British of all kinds of "fascist atrocities" committed against Hong Kong Chinese, collusion with United States imperialist aggression in Vietnam, and "repeated military and police maneuvers hostile to China."[56] Furthermore, some of these statements suggested that the time had finally come for the Chinese masses to confront and defeat British colonialism in Hong Kong:

> British imperialism is the extremely vicious ruler of Hong Kong, the enemy of the four million Chinese compatriots there and the enemy of 700 million Chinese people. For more than a hundred years, this moribund, savage imperialism has subjected our compatriots in Hong Kong and Kowloon to brutal oppression. . . . By plundering and bleeding our compatriots

white, British imperialism has plunged the broad masses of them into a state of impoverishment. . . . British imperialism has done so much evil, incurred so many blood debts and committed such towering crimes, these accounts must be settled."[57]

The earliest of the editorials also pledged support for the movement to "settle accounts" in Hong Kong. By mid-summer, however, the Chinese had retreated from this position. Official statements emphasized that any settling of blood debts would be carried out by Hong Kong residents themselves, not by their mainland compatriots. No liberating force would be sent to the colony. After initial expressions of support, PRC statements called for the colony's leftists to focus their energies on organizing and educating local residents instead of attacking the Hong Kong government, an indication that the conditions for recovery of the colony were not yet considered ripe. The Chinese also refused to make additional funds available to the Struggle Committee when it ran into financial difficulties in the fall of 1967. The PRC's boldest move, cutting food shipments, was halted after four days. Despite the refusal to fulfill requests for additional water supplies, the colony's normal water supply was continued without interruption,[58] and a new water agreement was reached in October.

It is important to note that the initiative for the disturbances came from within Hong Kong, and that at least some top CCP leaders tried to limit the disruption. As early as October 1966, Zhou Enlai had warned that the Cultural Revolution in Hong Kong was to be peaceful and was not meant to liberate the colony.[59] Later, Zhou was to be a strong advocate of keeping Hong Kong's protests limited and was reportedly supported in this regard by Mao Zedong.[60] A proposal to send four hundred specially-trained Red Guards to Hong Kong, favored by radical elements in the government, was reportedly opposed by Zhou and Defense Minister Lin Biao. It was also reported that secret talks between Hong Kong authorities and the PLA in August resulted in agreements that removed the risk of escalation of the violence.[61] Chinese troops at the Hong Kong border on several occasions clashed with groups of Red Guards who attempted to force their way into the colony in order to stage demonstrations there,[62] and authorities in Canton reportedly warned that anyone caught attempting to cross the border would be arrested and punished. A circular from the Canton Military Area Command criticized the events in Hong Kong as "leftist adventurism" and warned mass organizations in Guangdong not to support such activities.[63] PRC ships were the first to break the Hong Kong Seamen's Union boycott as disturbances drew to a close in September 1967, and the leftist violence, which had begun internally, was finally ended by a CCP directive.[64] At the end of October, the PRC's top officials in Hong Kong, from the Bank of China, China Resources, NCNA and other organizations, were called to Beijing and reportedly criticized for allowing matters to get out of hand in the colony.[65]

The events of the Cultural Revolution in Hong Kong in part reflect ongoing struggles among the PRC's central leadership over the direction of the Cultural Revolution in the mainland. Leftist leaders in the colony would probably not have taken such dramatic measures without some indication of support from Beijing, and extreme leftist members of the PRC's top leadership were probably pleased to see British authority in Hong Kong challenged. Nevertheless, the highest members of the Chinese leadership, including Mao, Lin and Zhou, supported the status quo in Hong Kong and were determined that violent disturbances not challenge British administration there. Not long after the disruption ended, CCP members in Hong Kong reportedly received explicit instructions reminding them that the PRC's policy did not include recovery of Hong Kong in the near future.[66]

Understanding Chinese Policy

Before and after 1949, the CCP's official position regarding Hong Kong was characterized by virulent opposition to the British presence there. This reflects the importance of anti-imperialism to the Communist movement as well as the differences in political and economic orientation between the PRC and its colonial neighbor. On several occasions after 1949, PRC officials expressed in unequivocal terms their opposition to British colonialism in Hong Kong and criticized certain policies adopted by the Hong Kong government. Nevertheless, like the Nationalists before them, the Communists adopted an accommodative approach toward Hong Kong. PRC leaders were reluctant to stir up controversy that would destabilize Hong Kong and were determined to reassure the British that the colony's status was not threatened. This continued to be true in spite of Hong Kong's extreme vulnerability to the mainland. Hong Kong's survival during this period depended increasingly not only on the PRC's acquiescence, but on its cooperation.

Beginning in the 1950s, the CCP's Hong Kong policy was reportedly based on "planning on a long term basis and full utilization." This meant that, on the one hand, no measures should be taken to affect Hong Kong's status in the foreseeable future, while on the other hand, full advantage should be taken of the colony's benefits to the mainland. In support of this approach, Mao Zedong is reported to have said in 1959: "We had better not recover Hong Kong in the near future. There is no hurry. Hong Kong is of use to us at present." In the early 1960s, amidst economic crisis on the mainland, Zhou Enlai ordered supplies to Hong Kong to be maintained, because "guaranteeing supplies to Hong Kong is in fact a political task."[67]

If previous Chinese governments had lacked the military might to take Hong Kong by force, this was not an important constraint for the Communist government after 1949. The British would not have been able to resist a Chinese invasion without substantial reinforcements, perhaps including assistance from the U.S. Seventh Fleet, and even then the Chinese could have cut off crucial supplies to the colony, including food and water. Conventional wisdom in Hong Kong has long held that leaders in Beijing could take back the colony simply by making a telephone call. While this is an exaggeration, it expresses a vulnerability to the PRC that Hong Kong's leaders recognized increasingly after 1949, but which was difficult to prevent.

Incentives for the Chinese to take back Hong Kong by force have not been strong, however. As in much of the twentieth century, domestic and foreign policy matters of more immediate importance continued to overshadow the Hong Kong question. In the years immediately following the establishment of the PRC, when the rationale for recovering the colony might have been strongest, Beijing was far more concerned with the KMT in Taiwan as its primary reunification question, and the PRC soon was entangled in the Korean War. Statements made by Chinese officials in 1950 proclaimed that all of China had been liberated except Tibet and Taiwan, ignoring Hong Kong and Macau and suggesting that they were in a different category.[68] In an interview in 1961, Chinese Foreign Minister Chen Yi said, "We must first resolve the most important problem, Taiwan. And then, at the opportune moment, we will claim Macau and Hong Kong."[69]

China's restraint toward Hong Kong, as in other foreign policy areas, was further influenced by its desire for respect in the international arena. Like the Nationalists, the Communists were eager to show their willingness to act "responsibly." Except for a period of extreme radicalism in 1967, the Chinese government has been anxious not to allow the British presence in Hong Kong to stand in the way of the development of Sino-British relations. Chinese leaders have further recognized that any disruptive actions toward the colony taken for the sake of asserting Chinese sovereignty would only bring condemnation from the West and damage more important foreign policy goals.

Beijing also valued the benefits it derived from Hong Kong's status as a British colony, including its role as a "door to the world." Beginning in the early 1950s, Hong Kong became an important location for contacts, particularly concerning trade, with Western and other Asian countries. Its excellent communications infrastructure, relatively modern and Westernized environment, and easy access from around the world made Hong Kong a convenient location for a variety of activities, including external propaganda, intelligence gathering, business negotiations and informal diplomatic contacts.

The relatively open atmosphere in Hong Kong had its drawbacks from the Communist perspective, of course, including the presence of the Nationalists' own intelligence and propaganda organs. There is some indication, though, that the Communists accepted this tradeoff as long as activities in the colony posed no subversive threat to the mainland. In an off-the-record interview with a Reuters correspondent in December 1948, the CCP's spokesman in Hong Kong, Qiao Guanhua, explained:

> The British government's policy of neutrality in China's civil war and the hospitality extended to the Communists in Hong Kong is greatly appreciated. The British authorities' statement that they would not permit Hong Kong to be used as a base of operations against the government of China was welcome as it is hoped that this policy will continue when the Communists and other liberal groups become China's recognized government. The Communists could understand the Hong Kong Government's policy if the Nationalist leaders should become refugees in the colony, as the latter's position would then be the same as the Communists' present position. The Chinese Communists could have perfectly normal relations with the United Kingdom.[70]

Of all the benefits that the mainland gained from Hong Kong, the one that grew most dramatically during this period was economic. As Hong Kong developed from a predominantly entrepôt economy to a manufacturing center and later a financial center, and as the mainland's modernization slowly moved ahead, economic ties between the PRC and Hong Kong increased at a steady rate. The PRC profited enormously from this relationship, acquiring an irreplaceable source of foreign exchange that at one point exceeded fifty percent of its total foreign exchange earnings and remained between 30 and 40 percent throughout the 1980s. Beginning in 1952, the bilateral trade balance was in China's favor every year, and by the end of 1976 it totalled almost US$12 billion. The Chinese economy also gained from millions of parcels of clothes and foodstuffs, along with sums of money, that Hong Kong residents sent to poorer mainland relatives and friends, amounting to US$2.4 billion between 1950 and 1976.[71] Expenditures by Hong Kong visitors to China between 1961 and 1976 totalled another US$973 million. The Chinese also increased their financial involvement in the colony, and by 1976 had five insurance companies and 13 banks with 113 branches there.[72]

One should be careful not to overemphasize the economic motives behind Chinese policy, however. Chinese earnings from Hong Kong did not begin to grow significantly until the late 1950s, well after Beijing's policy on Hong Kong had been established. In addition, other considerations, particularly foreign policy concerns, provided sufficiently compelling reasons to insure Hong Kong's safety. By acquiescing to the British presence in Hong Kong, Chinese leaders avoided an unnecessary and potentially damaging international dispute, while at the same time gaining the benefits generated by a successful colony on their doorstep. The only cost for this approach was an apparent contradiction of the Communists' own stated principles on regaining China's territorial integrity, but that issue was solved simply by postponing it. Tao Zhu, governor and first party secretary of Guangdong, put the matter aptly to Hong Kong and Macau members of the Guangdong session of the CPPCC in 1956: "Is it not beneficial to all concerned if there is friendship between Guangdong and Hong Kong and Macau?"[73]

Notes

1. I. S. Ojha, *Chinese Foreign Policy in an Age of Transition: The Diplomacy of Despair* (Boston: Beacon Press, 1969), quoted in Alan Lawrance, *China's Foreign Relations Since 1949* (London: Routledge and Kegan Paul, 1975): 246.

2. Gary Catron, *China and Hong Kong, 1949–1967* (Ph.D. Dissertation, Harvard University, 1971): 92, 72–73.

3. Catron, *China and Hong Kong*, 70, 101–5.

4. Mao Zedong, "The Chinese Revolution and the Chinese Communist Party," *Selected Works of Mao Tse-tung*, vol. 2 (Beijing: Foreign Languages Press, 1965): 311–18.

5. Mao Zedong, "On the People's Democratic Dictatorship," *Selected Works of Mao Tse-Tung*, vol. 4: 417.

6. Harold C. Hinton, ed., *The People's Republic of China, 1949–1979: A Documentary Survey*, vol. 1 (Wilmington, Del.: Scholarly Resources, Inc., 1980): 51, 55.

7. William L. Tung, *China and the Foreign Powers: The Impact of and Reaction to Unequal Treaties* (Dobbs Ferry, N.Y.: Oceana Publications, 1970): 301.

8. The British government claimed the Amethyst's mission on the Yangtze was peaceful, but the Chinese accused Britain of attempting to meddle in Chinese internal affairs and held the gunboat for three months before it was able to escape. See Catron, *China and Hong Kong*, 103–4.

9. Hungdah Chiu, "A Comparison of the Nationalist and Communist Views of Unequal Treaties," in Jerome Alan Cohen, ed., *China's Practice of International Law: Some Case Studies* (Cambridge: Harvard University Press, 1972): 258.

10. Shi Sung, Yu Daxin, Lu Yinghui and Cao Ke, "An Initial Investigation into the Old Law Viewpoint in the Teaching of International Law," *Jiaoxue yu Yanjiu* [Teaching and Research], no. 4 (1958): 15–16, in Jerome Alan Cohen and

Hungdah Chiu, *People's China and International Law: A Documentary Study* (Princeton: Princeton University Press, 1974): 335.

11. Xin Wu, " A Criticism of Bourgeois International Law on the Question of State Territory," *Guoji Wenti Yanjiu* [Studies in International Problems], no. 7 (1960): 44–51, in Cohen and Chiu, *People's China*, 326.

12. Xin Wu, "A Criticism," 331.

13. *People's Daily*, March 8, 1963, quoted in Cohen and Chiu, *People's China*, 380–81.

14. Catron, *China and Hong Kong*, 228.

15. *South China Morning Post*, Dec. 13, 1962; *TASS*, May 5, 1964, in Dennis J. Doolin, *Territorial Claims in the Sino-Soviet Conflict* (Stanford: Stanford University Press, 1965): 41.

16. *New China News Agency*, September 25, 1964, quoted in Cohen and Chiu, *People's China*, 381–82.

17. Quoted in Cohen and Chiu, *People's China*, 384.

18. *People's Daily*, October 26, 1955, quoted in Cohen and Chiu, *People's China*, 376.

19. J. P. Jain, *China in World Politics: A Study of Sino-British Relations, 1949–1975* (New Delhi: Radiant Publishers, 1976): 166.

20. Catron, *China and Hong Kong*, 245.

21. Gene Gleason, *Hong Kong* (London: Robert Hale Ltd., 1963): 87.

22. Catron, *China and Hong Kong*, 242–43.

23. Catron, *China and Hong Kong*, 166, 189.

24. Gary Catron, "Hong Kong and Chinese Foreign Policy, 1955–1960," *China Quarterly* 51 (July-Sept. 1972): 406–7.

25. Jain, *China*, 183.

26. *Foreign Relations of the United States*, 1949, vol. 7: 515.

27. *Foreign Relations*, 1949, vol. 7: 481.

28. *Foreign Relations*, 1949, vol. 7: 538.

29. *Foreign Relations*, 1949, vol. 7: 577.

30. Catron, *China and Hong Kong*, 107–8.

31. *Xianggang yu Zhongguo: Lishi Wenjian Ziliao Huibian* [Hong Kong and China: A Collection of Historical Documents and Materials] (Hong Kong: Wide Angle Press, 1981): 226–27.

32. Catron, *China and Hong Kong*, 115.

33. Catron, *China and Hong Kong*, 115–16.

34. Catron, *China and Hong Kong*, 118.

35. *Xianggang yu Zhongguo*, 227–28.

36. Catron, "Chinese Foreign Policy," 407–8.

37. Catron, "Chinese Foreign Policy," 407.

38. *Hong Kong 1962* (Hong Kong: Government Printer, 1963): 211–12.

39. Gleason, *Hong Kong*, 79–83.

40. Jain, *China*, 174.

41. Jain, *China*, 175.

42. Catron, "Chinese Foreign Policy," 413.

43. Jain, *China*, 174.

44. *Qishi Niandai* [The Seventies], no. 12 (Dec. 1, 1982): 27–30, in Foreign Broadcast Information Service [FBIS], *Daily Report: China*, Dec. 6, 1982, W2.

45. Catron, "Chinese Foreign Policy," 414–15.

46. Catron, *China and Hong Kong*, 115.

47. Peter Wesley-Smith, *Unequal Treaty 1898–1997: China, Great Britain and Hong Kong* (Hong Kong: Oxford University Press, 1980): 128.

48. *New China News Agency*, Jan. 17, 1963, quoted in Cohen and Chiu, *People's China*, 378.

49. Catron, *China and Hong Kong*, 237.

50. Wesley-Smith, *Unequal Treaty*, 128.

51. For details of the riots and related issues, see John Cooper, *Colony in Conflict May 1967–January 1968* (Hong Kong: Swindon Book Co., 1970).

52. Jain, *China*, 176–77.

53. John D. Young, "China's Role in Two Hong Kong Disturbances: A Scenario for the Future?," *Journal of Oriental Studies* 19, no. 2 (1981): 161.

54. Young, "China's Role," 167.

55. Jain, *China*, 177–78.

56. Statement of the Chinese Ministry of Foreign Affairs, May 15, 1967, quoted in *The May Upheaval in Hong Kong* (Hong Kong: Committee of Hong Kong–Kowloon Chinese Compatriots for the Struggle Against Persecution by the British Authorities in Hong Kong, 1967): 146.

57. Quoted in *May Upheaval*, 146.

58. *Far Eastern Economic Review Yearbook, 1968* (Hong Kong: Far Eastern Economic Review Ltd.); Jain, *China*, 178.

59. Catron, *Hong Kong and China*, 292.

60. Professor Wang Tieya, Beijing University, personal communication, January 1984.

61. Melvin Gurtov and Byong-Moo Hwang, *China Under Threat: The Politics of Strategy and Diplomacy*, (Baltimore: The Johns Hopkins University Press, 1980): 207.

62. *Far Eastern Economic Review Yearbook, 1968*: 167.

63. Jürgen Domes, "The Impact of the Hong Kong Problem and Agreement on PRC Domestic Politics," in Jürgen Domes and Yu-ming Shaw, eds., *Hong Kong: A Chinese and International Concern* (Boulder: Westview Press, 1988): 85.

64. Catron, *China and Hong Kong*, 306, 310.

65. L. F. Goodstadt, "Day of Reckoning," *Far Eastern Economic Review*, 58, no. 6 (Nov. 9, 1967): 293–95.

66. *Qishi Niandai*, in FBIS, Dec. 6, 1982, W3.

67. *Qishi Niandai*, in FBIS, Dec. 6, 1982, W1.

68. Evan Luard, *Britain and China*, (London: Chatto and Windus, 1962): 186.

69. Catron, *China and Hong Kong*, 230–31.

70. *Foreign Relations*, 1948, vol. 7: 660.

71. These remittances declined during the Cultural Revolution, apparently due to fears of Red Guard retaliation against recipients. In October 1966, however, it was rumored that Chinese authorities were trying to reassure Hong Kong and Overseas Chinese that the remittances would cause no harm, in order to maintain

that source of foreign currency. See *Far Eastern Economic Review Yearbook, 1967:* 171.

72. Y. C. Jao, "Hong Kong's Role in Financing China's Modernization," in A. J. Youngson, ed., *Hong Kong and China: The Economic Nexus* (Hong Kong: Oxford University Press, 1982): 40–44.

73. Catron, "Chinese Foreign Policy," 405.

5

Modernization, Reunification and the PRC's Hong Kong Policy After Mao

After Mao Zedong's death in 1976 and the emergence of Deng Xiaoping as China's paramount leader in 1978, substantive changes took place in Chinese politics and economics, with serious implications for the PRC's relationship with Hong Kong. The country embarked on a modernization drive fueled by reforms of the domestic economy and substantial reliance on foreign technology, capital and expertise. Relations with the United States and other capitalist countries improved, followed by a warming of the Sino-Soviet relationship. Chinese willingness to welcome foreign assistance and investment and to tolerate certain "negative" foreign influences, albeit with some setbacks, increased dramatically.

Hong Kong was uniquely positioned to take a leading role in cooperating with the PRC's modernization drive. Because of their close ties with the language, culture and geography of the mainland, Hong Kong entrepreneurs were able to provide capital and expertise for joint-venture projects on the mainland. The colony also became an increasingly important location for PRC trade, investment and training. These developments increased Hong Kong's value to the Beijing leadership at precisely the moment the colony's future status was brought into serious doubt.

Sovereignty and Modernization

The Third Plenum of the CCP's Eleventh Central Committee in December 1978 marked Deng Xiaoping's ascension to the top of the Chinese leadership and the PRC's embarkation on a path of economic reform and cooperation with the West. Without sacrificing the principle of national independence, the plenum established modernization as the nation's primary goal. In order to achieve the Four Modernizations (in agriculture, industry, science and technology, and national defense) by the end of the century, the PRC would maintain an "open door," learning from developed countries and purchasing their technology.

Recognizing the benefits that Hong Kong had provided Chinese development in the past, the new leadership headed by Deng expected the colony to play a key role in this process. In 1978 the State Council established its own Hong Kong and Macau Affairs Office, organizationally distinct from the Hong Kong and Macau Affairs Office under the Ministry of Foreign Affairs, with the primary task of working on Hong Kong policy. In November 1978, the Chinese vice-minister of foreign affairs confirmed that Hong Kong and Macau were "of interest" to the PRC in its modernization drive and would continue to receive the mainland's support.[1] In Hong Kong a month later, Foreign Trade Minister Li Qiang asked for the territory's assistance in the Four Modernizations, calling its role "significant" and suggesting that the mainland could learn much from studying Hong Kong.[2] In March 1980, Wang Kuang, director of NCNA's Hong Kong branch (which serves as the PRC's unofficial embassy in the colony), called for greater contact between Hong Kong and the mainland in order to aid the PRC's modernization.[3] A similar message was delivered to Sir Phillip Haddon-Cave, Hong Kong financial secretary, during his visit to the mainland in 1980,[4] and to numerous Hong Kong businessmen in the following months.

The PRC's intention to rely on Hong Kong was underscored in March 1979, when Hong Kong Governor Sir Murray MacLehose travelled to Beijing at the invitation of Foreign Trade Minister Li. In what was a significant concession for the Chinese, who had previously referred to the colony's officials as "British authorities in Hong Kong," MacLehose was invited as "the governor of Hong Kong." In meetings with the governor, Chinese officials reasserted their hope that Hong Kong would play a major role in China's modernization and that trade relations would expand. Li was direct: "I will say what I said last year: I hope that our friends in Hong Kong will invest in China."[5] As to the colony's future status in light of the impending expiration of the New Territories lease, however, Chinese officials were unwilling to state their intentions publicly. It was later reported that Deng Xiaoping told MacLehose in private that the PRC would announce its intention to recover Hong Kong if the issue were raised publicly.[6] It appears, however, that the Chinese government had not yet considered the matter in detail. Publicly, Deng Xiaoping simply asked MacLehose to tell Hong Kong's residents to "set their hearts at ease."[7]

Though national reunification was one of the PRC's top stated policy goals, Chinese officials avoided the issue of Hong Kong's future, at times insisting that Hong Kong would be recovered only after Taiwan. The concept of an autonomous "administrative region" was developed by late 1978 as a proposal for Taiwan's reunification with the mainland. In January 1979, Deng Xiaoping told a visiting delegation from the U.S. Senate Military Affairs Committee that after its proposed reunification, Taiwan would remain completely autonomous, retaining its administrative power, security forces, and social and economic systems.[8] But the concept had apparently not yet been applied to Hong Kong. In May, responding to an inquiry from a delegation of French journalists, Vice Foreign Minister Song Zhiguang took the well-known official position that "Hong Kong is a part of China" and "when the lease expires, an appropriate attitude would be adopted in settling the question."[9]

By October 1979 the Chinese at least were willing to acknowledge that talks would have to take place to discuss Hong Kong's future, though they did not say when. Premier Hua Guofeng, before leaving for a trip to Europe, told a press conference:

> China's position with regard to the Xianggang [Hong Kong] question has been very clear. When Vice-Premier Deng Xiaoping met with the Governor of Xianggang, he reiterated our attitude. Currently, our relations with the United Kingdom and the British authorities in Xianggang are quite good. As to questions relating to Xianggang, Jiulong [Kowloon] and the New Territories, we think that a good way of settling the question can be sought through consultations. But I think regardless of how the matter is settled, we will take notice of the interests of investors there.[10]

In a visit to London a year later, Foreign Minister Huang Hua assured the British that they need not worry about Hong Kong's future and stressed that the questions of Hong Kong, Kowloon and the New Territories could be settled through negotiations.[11]

The same message appeared in a November 1980 interview given by Zhao Guanqi, director of the State Council's Bureau of Government Offices Administration, to a Hong Kong journal. Zhao said the Hong Kong problem should be solved slowly through consultations. He emphasized that Hong Kong had made great contributions to the mainland and that it would benefit all concerned if the status quo were maintained. "Our government recognizes that whatever solution [is arrived at] for the future of Hong Kong, it must not materially change the livelihood of the people of Hong Kong," he said. "Indeed, any instability that may visit Hong Kong will be detrimental to us too." Zhao blamed Hong Kong's riots during the Cultural Revolution on "ultraleftist violence" and claimed that Mao Zedong and Zhou Enlai never would have authorized a takeover of Hong Kong because they recognized its importance to China.[12]

Deng Xiaoping provided similar assurances. In April 1981, he told British Foreign Secretary Lord Carrington that China's stated policy toward Hong Kong's status would not change, and he called for greater economic cooperation between China and Britain.[13] In July, Deng told Louis Cha, chairman and president of the Hong Kong newspaper *Ming Pao*, that China's three goals were to fight hegemonism and safeguard world peace, unify the country, and work for economic construction. He stressed that the third goal took precedence over the other two, an indication that Hong Kong's future status would be resolved in a manner consistent with its provision of economic benefit to the mainland.[14]

These statements amount to little more than a reiteration of long-held principles regarding the Hong Kong question. They suggest that, even by mid–1981, the PRC's leadership had not developed a detailed plan for Hong Kong's future. It was increasingly apparent, however, that such a plan could not be avoided. The issue of Hong Kong's future status and China's claim to sovereignty finally had appeared on the agenda of Chinese leaders, just as they began to exploit the colony's potential to assist China's modernization.

Increased Contact with the Colony

The years following the reappearance of Deng Xiaoping at the top of the Chinese leadership saw tremendous expansion in contacts between the PRC and Hong Kong. This trend had begun in the early 1970s, but under the new modernization drive its pace increased dramatically. Direct communications and travel links opened between Hong Kong and China's major cities and large numbers of Hong Kong residents began to travel in the mainland. Both sides sent delegations—in sports, culture, academics, politics and other areas—that further strengthened the ties. High-level contacts between government officials became increasingly common. Mainland universities reopened to Hong Kong, Macau and Taiwan "compatriots," as did mainland cemeteries. Cooperation on bilateral issues, such as illegal immigrants, also improved.

The PRC expanded noticeably its investments in the colony, which previously had centered on shipping, transport, distribution and finance. By the early 1980s, its interests included a cigarette factory, real estate companies, a chain of department stores selling mainland products, warehouse and cold storage facilities, a major travel agency, an airline office, book stores, printing presses, periodicals, gasoline stations and a large trading organization, China Resources, which organized Chinese trade through the colony.[15] The Chinese also ran several passenger transport services to the mainland, including a virtual monopoly on all flights to major Chinese cities, and controlled a major shipping line.

The thirteen mainland banks in Hong Kong operated almost 200 branches and were involved in two other joint-venture commercial banks. In 1978 Beijing authorized those banks to invest in shares, bonds, gold and other commodities, as well as foreign currencies and real estate, allowing them to play a much larger role in the colony's local economy. The PRC also owned five insurance companies in the colony and had entered into a number of major joint ventures with Hong Kong investors for projects both in the mainland and in Hong Kong.[16] In 1979, China and Hong Kong signed a ten-year contract for the supply of coal to the colony's Lamma power station.[17] They also completed an agreement that increased the mainland's supply of water to the colony. Trade in both directions continued to grow: between 1976 and 1981 the value of Hong Kong's domestic exports to China multiplied 120 times. The amount of Chinese goods re-exported from Hong Kong reached thirty-one percent of the territory's total in 1981.[18]

This blossoming relationship was soon to be disturbed, however. By the middle of 1982 it was clear to the Chinese leadership that, due to the march of time and the legitimate concerns of Hong Kong investors, the "Hong Kong question" could no longer be avoided publicly.

The Debate Begins

"Hong Kong is a problem left over from history and we are not eager to tackle it."[19] This statement, made in 1979 by the head of the China Products Company, sums up well the Chinese perspective on Hong Kong, particularly with modernization efforts proceeding full steam on the mainland. Nevertheless, history was catching up with Hong Kong, and the Chinese would be forced to tackle the question.

As the 1980s approached, it became apparent that repayment periods for mortgages in the New Territories would soon begin to extend beyond 1997. This prospect left investors uneasy. The Hong Kong government also faced a legal quandary, since it was unable to lease land for periods after which its own rights would cease. It was this impending deadline that led Hong Kong businessmen to bring their concerns to the Hong Kong government, and Governor MacLehose to raise the issue with Deng Xiaoping in Beijing.

It is important to understand that the initiative in this case came from the British and Hong Kong side, not from the Chinese government, which remained reluctant to confront the question. Considerable attention has been given to the notion that the British might have simply ignored the deadline, allowing the two sides to play indefinitely a game of diplomatic postponement. The legal requirements on the British side, however, were such that ignoring the treaty's deadline would not have set the hearts of Hong Kong businessmen at ease. In terms Chinese officials had long used, conditions had become "ripe" for resolution of the Hong Kong question, whether the British and Chinese liked it or not.

Once raised publicly, the Hong Kong question took on a new character. The Chinese were increasingly pressured to explain in detail their plans for the colony's status as a reintegrated part of the motherland. Thus by June 1982, Deng Xiaoping was willing to tell a group of Hong Kong and Macau community leaders that, as a matter of principle, the PRC would reassert its sovereignty "sometime about 1997," but would do so in a manner designed to maintain the territory's stability and prosperity and to allow Hong Kong to function as a free port.[20]

The first legal provision for Hong Kong's reintegration appeared in the 1982 National Constitution, which referred to Special Administrative Regions. Clearly directed at integrating Hong Kong, Macau and eventually Taiwan back into the mainland, Article 31 of the constitution reads, "The State may establish Special Administrative Regions where necessary. The systems to be instituted in Special Administrative Regions shall be prescribed by law and enacted by the National People's Congress in the light of the specific conditions."

Peng Zhen, then vice-chairman of the Standing Committee of the National People's Congress (NPC) and vice-chairman of the National Constitution Revision Committee, explained that Article 31 provided a "legal basis for the peaceful reunification of the motherland."[21] From Hong Kong's perspective, however, Article 31 looked like less of a breakthrough. As a broad statement of Chinese intentions, it was too vague to inspire confidence in the future, and its reference to the NPC appeared to sacrifice local autonomy to the ultimate authority of Beijing.

Chinese officials had already begun to think in more specific terms, however. The July 1982 issue of the Hong Kong journal, *Cheng Ming*, revealed the major elements of Beijing's position. It stated that the treaties relating to Hong Kong were unequal and that Hong Kong and Macau rightfully belonged under Chinese sovereignty. Furthermore, regaining sovereignty was "not something in the remote future." China would adopt a "one country, two systems," approach to solve the problem of Hong Kong. Its capitalist system would not be changed and it would remain a free port.[22] Soon thereafter an article in the PRC's *Workers' Daily* said that a peaceful solution to the problem would be reached that would maintain Hong Kong's prosperity.[23] In August, information was leaked indicating that, after the Chinese regained sovereignty in Hong Kong, its governor would be an appointed or elected local official, the first specific reference to the nature of the PRC's plans for Hong Kong's "autonomy" after 1997.[24]

With these developments, the government in Beijing had quietly made known the fundamental elements of its approach to the emerging issue of Hong Kong's future—recovery of sovereignty, accompanied by unusual steps to allow Hong Kong to govern itself—thus setting the stage for Prime Minister Margaret Thatcher's visit to Beijing in September 1982. At the end of August, Chinese Vice–Foreign Minister Qian Qichen reiterated that Hong Kong "is part of Chinese territory" and its occupation by the British is a "historical problem." However, he explained, "What is happening is that a lot of people have material and financial interests in Hong Kong." The PRC's goal was to reassert its sovereignty without harming those interests.[25]

The Thatcher Visit and After

A Hard-Line Stance on Sovereignty

Prime Minister Thatcher apparently failed to recognize the seriousness of the Chinese commitment to regaining sovereignty in Hong Kong and the rancor with which Chinese leaders regarded the unequal treaties. When she met with Deng Xiaoping and Premier Zhao Ziyang during the first official visit of a British prime minister to Beijing, she insisted on British sovereignty in the colony and on the validity of the treaties that had ceded and leased the colony to the British.

This was a position that the Chinese were simply unwilling to accept. Deng Xiaoping reportedly said that he refused to be a second Li Hongzhang, a reference to the viceroy of Guangdong who signed away the New Territories in 1898. Just before a second session of talks with Thatcher was to begin, Zhao announced to a group of British journalists that sovereignty was not negotiable. He recognized that there was concern within Hong Kong about reassertion of Chinese sovereignty. However, he argued, the colony's residents had nothing to fear, because the Chinese would take measures to "guarantee Hong Kong's prosperity and stability." "I believe problems of this kind are not difficult to solve," he said, "as long as both sides approach and develop Sino-British relations in a long-term strategic perspective."[26]

Thatcher flew from Beijing to Hong Kong, where she reiterated her position that the treaties regarding Hong Kong were valid in international law, asserting that any government that failed to honor one set of treaties could not be trusted to honor others. She also insisted that Great Britain had a "moral responsibility and duty" to the people of Hong Kong. To PRC leaders, these statements were a slap in the face. They had fought for decades to achieve the abrogation of unequal treaties, and Thatcher now claimed that the treaties were legally valid. They had also struggled to gain respect for China as a responsible actor in the world arena, and Thatcher was now calling the Chinese government untrustworthy. Finally, the Beijing government had always considered Chinese residents in Hong Kong to be "compatriots" living temporarily under British rule, rather than British subjects, and now Thatcher was suggesting that those residents needed British protection against possibly harmful Chinese actions. (Ironically, the British commitment to Hong Kong residents was severely restricted by the passage in 1981 of a British Nationality Act that denied Hong Kong residents right of abode in Britain.)

The Chinese response to Thatcher's statements was swift and strong. In a highly critical article entitled "China's Stand on Hong Kong Issue Is Solemn and Just," NCNA lashed out at the British position, asserting that the Chinese government and people had never accepted the unequal treaties.

> These treaties, which were forced upon the Chinese people, provide an ironclad proof of British imperialism's plunder of Chinese territory. The Chinese people have always held that these treaties are illegal and therefore null and void. Even when they were still in a powerless status, the Chinese people waged a protracted, unremitting and heroic struggle against imperialist humiliation and oppression and against the series of unequal treaties forced upon them by imperialism. It was not until the founding of the People's Republic of China in 1949 that the Chinese people finally won independence and emancipation. Now that the Chinese people have stood up, it is only natural that they find these treaties . . . unacceptable.[27]

The article argued further that, since Hong Kong was Chinese territory, only the PRC government, "as the government of a sovereign country," had responsibility or duty regarding Hong Kong's Chinese residents. At the same time, however, NCNA pointed out that consultations on the future of Hong Kong were to continue through diplomatic channels "in light of bilateral aims of preserving the stability and prosperity of Hong Kong."[28]

The Chinese and British had agreed on the maintenance of Hong Kong's "stability and prosperity" as their common goal in negotiating Hong Kong's future, and the terms were to become the watchwords of official statements thereafter. Like many diplomatic phrases, this one papered over as much as it revealed. The British were interested not only in stability and prosperity but in playing an administrative role in Hong Kong after 1997. The Chinese were anxious to maintain stability and prosperity, but not at the expense of sovereignty. And for many Hong Kong residents, who were left without formal representation at the Sino-British talks, the twin goals of stability and prosperity sounded reasonable but hollow; to them the territory's way of life was comprised of much more than political quietude and a rising stock market index.

Talks Begin: A Plan Revealed

The Sino-British negotiations on Hong Kong's future began in October 1982 and continued for two years. The two sides agreed from the outset to maintain strict secrecy, but frequent statements by Chinese officials revealed the progress of the talks and provided an increasingly clear picture of Chinese plans. As preliminary discussions began, an unnamed Chinese Foreign Ministry official told a team of *Financial Times* reporters that sovereignty took precedence over prosperity and that as soon as the former was regained, "special measures" would be taken to guarantee the latter. He said there would be no less freedom in Hong Kong after China regained control and that it was possible British "experts" could participate in the territory's administration, though ultimate authority would reside in Beijing.[29]

In early November, the Chinese government announced that a plan for the transfer of authority in Hong Kong should be completed within two years, thereby imposing a unilateral deadline on the talks.[30] This put pressure on the British side, which did not want to be forced to make last-minute concessions to meet an artificial deadline. The move appears to have been more than a negotiating tactic, however. The PRC was anxious to resolve the question of Hong Kong's future quickly in order to preserve the territory's stability, to prevent the British from building popular support in Hong Kong for their own negotiating position, and to give itself an influential role during the long transition period. The two-year limit had the additional advantage of underlining the PRC's claim that it had the ultimate right to determine Hong Kong's future. The deadline was repeated on several occasions during the negotiations as a public reminder of this claim, but PRC officials never described in detail what their threatened unilateral declaration on Hong Kong's future would entail. After the two sides agreed on major points of principle, the PRC backed away from its deadline.

It was clear at this early stage that the PRC had worked out some of the key details of its post–1997 Hong Kong policy. Wang Kuang promised that "China won't touch Hong Kong for at least fifteen years."[31] In late November 1982, the head of the State Council's Hong Kong and Macau Affairs Office, Liao Chengzhi, explained to a group of visiting Hong Kong factory owners that Hong Kong's administration after 1997 would adhere to the principle of "Hong Kong people ruling Hong Kong." Like "stability and prosperity," this simple formula for Hong Kong's future was soon to become common parlance in discussions of the colony's future, though the details of its implementation remained unclear long after the Sino-British agreement was signed. Liao also stated that neither Hong Kong's lifestyle nor its status as a free port and financial center would be changed.[32]

The Sino-British talks on Hong Kong continued through the first half of 1983 in a deadlock. The major stumbling block was sovereignty: the Chinese insisted that the British concede that fundamental point before discussing any details, while the British were unwilling to give up their hard-line stance. After eight months of stalemate, however, Prime Minister Thatcher finally recognized what some British Foreign Office officials had argued from the start, and acquiesced to the Chinese view. In May 1983, she informed Premier Zhao Ziyang secretly that Britain would accept the Chinese position on sovereignty if a solution could be reached to insure Hong Kong's stability and prosperity. The Chinese accepted this approach, and a second phase of talks began in July.[33]

Meanwhile, the Chinese government mounted a United Front campaign to gain support for its policy in Hong Kong. Through private meetings and public propaganda, the government sought to convince Hong Kong residents of its intention to preserve the colony's way of life. Scores of businessmen, professionals, intellectuals, members of public interest groups and others visited Beijing, where PRC officials asserted repeatedly that the two basic elements of their policy—recovery of sovereignty and preservation of stability and prosperity—were consistent. Chinese officials also used these meetings to reveal more details of their plans for the colony's future. By courting public opinion in this way, they hoped to win early support for their proposals, smooth the transfer of authority and earn the allegiance of future Hong Kong SAR residents.

Dr. John Young, a lecturer at Hong Kong University, returned from Beijing in May 1983 with the news that the territory would be ruled by Hong Kong residents, defined as "people who have lived in Hong Kong for seven years, accept Hong Kong as part of China and accept that China is the only legitimate Chinese government." These people would be responsible for administration of the SAR, which would have its own constitution. The delegation of academics of which Young was a member also reported that Beijing had drawn up contingency plans for taking over and maintaining stability in Hong Kong in case of a premature British withdrawal, which the Chinese considered a real possibility.[34] Liao Chengzhi reportedly told the academics that 1997 was the appropriate time to solve the Hong Kong problem and that Macau would be considered part of the same "entity." Liao also told a group of businessmen and industrialists in mid-May that Beijing would devise a practical plan for Hong Kong's future within two years, and that the Chinese would not simply march in and take back the territory.[35]

At meetings of the NPC and CPPCC in June and July, Deng Xiaoping reiterated that modernization was China's primary goal for the foreseeable future, indicating that other objectives, such as national reunification, were to be pursued in ways that contributed to modernization.[36] He told a Hong Kong delegate to the CPPCC that he hoped to see an agreement on Hong Kong reached within two years and that "a basic principle is to keep Hong Kong's prosperity."[37] According to Ho Yin, Chairman of the Macau Chamber of Commerce, Deng told him that the central government would not send anyone to govern Hong Kong after 1997. The territory would be governed by a resident of the colony who need not necessarily be Chinese.[38] It was also reported that Deng promised to protect foreign interests, especially British, after China regained sovereignty. He was more specific in a meeting with Winston Yang, an American academic, who said that Deng indicated Hong Kong would issue its own passports, maintain an independent judiciary and conduct internal affairs without interference from Beijing.[39]

At the end of July, a group of post-secondary schools students returned from the Chinese capital with a "ten-point plan," the most detailed explanation of Chinese intentions so far and an early foreshadowing of the agreement that would later be signed in Beijing. It included the following:

1. Except for issues affecting defense or diplomacy, Hong Kong would run its own affairs.
2. The territory would be ruled by a local government without Beijing's representation. The head of that government would be a "patriot," though not necessarily a socialist, who would be elected by Hong Kong citizens.
3. Hong Kong would make its own laws.
4. The colony's existing way of life would not be changed.
5. Crucial freedoms, including press, speech, assembly, and movement, would be retained.
6. Activities of political groups such as the KMT would not be restricted as long as they did not include sabotage.
7. The local police force would be responsible for security.
8. Hong Kong's capitalist system and status as a free port and financial center would not be altered.
9. The Hong Kong SAR would enjoy considerable autonomy from Beijing in its foreign relations and would issue its own travel documents.
10. Questions of social reform would be debated by the people of Hong Kong.[40]

The students were also told that Hong Kong residents could participate in drafting a proposal for the territory's governance, a "constitution" for Hong Kong, but that the document would have to be approved by the National People's Congress.[41] From the Chinese perspective, these ten points promised an unprecedented level of autonomy from the central government. Nevertheless, some aspects, particularly the ultimate authority of the NPC and the method of selecting Hong Kong's leaders, made Hong Kong residents uneasy, as would the agreement on Hong Kong's future and the draft Basic Law when they were completed some time later.

Chinese officials had always avoided specifying the date on which they would recover the colony, in part to avoid legitimizing the terms of the 1898 Convention of Beijing. Instead, they had insisted that because all three treaties concerning Hong Kong were invalid, the PRC could take back Hong Kong any time it wished. As the issue of Hong Kong's return became more concrete, however, the Chinese acquiesced on this matter of principle. Without explicitly granting legitimacy to the 1898 lease, CCP General Secretary Hu Yaobang told a Japanese journalist in August 1983 that the Chinese would recover the territory on July 1, 1997. In September 1983, Deng Xiaoping communicated the same message through former British Prime Minister Edward Heath.[42]

On the issue of formal sovereignty, however, the Chinese were unyielding. Officials in Beijing, particularly at the State Council's Hong Kong and Macau Affairs Office and in the Hong Kong and Macau Affairs Office of the Ministry of Foreign Affairs, paid close attention to events and public discourse in the colony. In the lively debate that followed Thatcher's visit to Beijing, several plans that were designed to allow the Chinese to recover nominal sovereignty but to continue British administration of Hong Kong were suggested in the Hong Kong press. Such plans attempted to reconcile two commonly recognized but incompatible notions: (1) that the British had taken Hong Kong by "unequal" treaties and that the Chinese claim to the territory therefore, on a fundamental level, was just, and (2) that Chinese residents of Hong Kong, even if they accepted the legitimacy of the Chinese claim to sovereignty and resented British colonial rule, nevertheless were reluctant to face the uncertainty that a transfer of sovereignty would entail. Under the circumstances, they preferred to keep things just as they were. A survey conducted in May-June 1982 by the Hong Kong Observers, a political pressure group, concluded that 95 percent of Hong Kong's population wanted to maintain the status quo after 1997. The prospect of returning the territory to Chinese sovereignty received the most "least preferred" and "not acceptable" responses.[43]

Sovereignty, Administration and the "Opinion Card"

The Chinese leadership regarded the publication of such survey results with suspicion. Always sensitive to perceived infringements on China's sovereignty (and concerned that the negotiations proceed as smoothly as possible), Chinese officials from the beginning had opposed any moves that might give Hong Kong residents influence at the bargaining table. They adamantly rejected British appeals for a "three-legged stool" approach to the negotiations. When Hong Kong Governor Sir Edward Youde announced that he would represent Hong Kong residents in the talks, the Chinese immediately rejected the idea, and Youde ultimately was welcomed in Beijing only as a member of the British delegation.

Furthermore, PRC officials felt that the British government was trying to strengthen its own hand in the negotiations by playing the "opinion card": publicizing the notion that Hong Kong residents were more concerned about maintaining the status quo in the colony than about achieving national reunification. These suspicions grew in part from a new deadlock that had emerged at the negotiating table since the second phase of talks had begun in July 1983. Having conceded sovereignty, Britain wanted to maintain a role in the territory's administration after 1997, but Chinese negotiators insisted that sovereignty and administration were indivisible. They were particularly annoyed by suggestions that Hong Kong's success was the result of British administration. In August and September 1983, NCNA fired off a volley of news reports and commentaries which argued that the hard work of Hong Kong residents and the supply of crucial commodities from the mainland, including water, food and oil, deserved most of the credit for Hong Kong's phenomenal growth.

The PRC further accused Great Britain of seeking a continuation of colonialism. A long article in *People's Daily* argued that since administration is "the power for the state to exercise its rule over the territory" and "a concrete exercise of sovereignty," it could not be separated from sovereignty. Therefore, an exchange of sovereignty for administration of the type that had been discussed in some circles was unacceptable. If China agreed to accept pro forma sovereignty while allowing the British to continue to administer Hong Kong, it would amount to signing "a new unequal treaty."[44]

One of the PRC's top legal experts, Shi Liang, argued that sovereignty and administration were inseparable, because "sovereignty means the supreme power inherent in a country in dealing with its internal affairs and international affairs without being interfered with or restrained by another country."[45] In other words, no matter what surveys in Hong Kong suggested about popular opinion (and several Chinese officials expressed doubt about the validity of such survey results), the legal nature of the relationship between sovereignty and administration precluded separating the two. NCNA wrote,

> . . . if administrative powers remain in British hands, how can China be said to have recovered sovereignty? In what sovereign state in the world is administrative power in the hands of foreigners? This absolutely cannot be determined by "public opinion" of any kind. No matter what "public opinion" says, if there is separation of sovereignty and administrative power, then there is no sovereignty. . . . We believe that prosperity and freedom are the greatest aspirations of the people of Hong Kong, but we also believe that the Chinese people of Hong Kong also have national integrity and will not be fooled by you in this way.[46]

Though such statements were generally greeted with alarm in Hong Kong, they were not intended to weaken Beijing's earlier promises. The PRC publication, *Banyue Tan* [Fortnightly Chats], in September 1983 repeated earlier pledges of guaranteed autonomy and continued prosperity, adding that the territory's local government would remain unchanged "for a long time." "We are fully confident that after the recovery of sovereignty over Hong Kong, Hong Kong compatriots will certainly administer Hong Kong still better."[47]

These assurances were not enough to calm Hong Kong's economic jitters, however. A steady decline in the value of the Hong Kong dollar became precipitous in September, after the fourth round of talks concluded without breaking the stalemate. The Chinese accused the British of deliberately creating the crisis and criticized the Hong Kong government for not taking measures to halt the currency's decline. On September 30, 1983, Ji Pengfei, who in June had succeeded Liao Chengzhi as director of the State Council's Hong Kong and Macau Affairs Office, repeated the earlier warning that the Chinese government was prepared to make a unilateral declaration of its plans for Hong Kong in September 1984 if no agreement could be reached with the British before that time.[48] Other statements accused the British of being too rigid in the negotiations and of attempting to block China's recovery of sovereignty.[49] In a statement that sent further chills through a colony whose stock market had become a barometer of China–Hong Kong relations, two members of the NPC Standing Committee suggested that China was prepared to assume sovereignty earlier than 1997 if Hong Kong's economy continued to decline.[50]

Under the circumstances, the Hong Kong government intervened to halt the crisis, eliminating the ten percent tax on Hong Kong dollar deposits and pegging the currency to the U.S. dollar. More important,

Thatcher sent another secret note to Zhao, finally conceding both sovereignty and administration after 1997. This cleared the way for the negotiations to move forward, and the following year was spent discussing the details of Hong Kong's post–1997 status.

China's highest officials and those closest to the Hong Kong issue continued to provide reassurances about the colony's future. General Secretary Hu Yaobang announced during a visit to Tokyo at the end of September that Japanese firms would be allowed to continue their operations unhindered after 1997.[51] Beijing had been concerned that foreigners might withdraw their investments if Hong Kong's future appeared insecure, and officials later continued to remind foreign governments of China's commitment to Hong Kong's prosperity.

More significant, in a meeting with Hong Kong Urban Councillor Dr. Denny Huang, Ji Pengfei offered a detailed outline of how the Hong Kong Special Administrative Region would operate. Ji agreed with Huang's suggestions that prompt steps be taken to secure Hong Kong's status as an SAR and that Hong Kong residents be consulted in the drafting of a constitution. As for China's post–1997 plans, Ji said Hong Kong would retain all its laws, except those "connected with colonial rule," and would have its own final court of appeal. China would be responsible for the territory's defense but would not station troops there (this later was changed). The Chinese central government would also be responsible for Hong Kong's overall external affairs, but the right to manage certain aspects of foreign relations (for example, the negotiation of trade agreements) would reside in the SAR. Hong Kong would also retain complete control over immigration matters, issuing its own identity cards and passports, and would handle its own foreign trade relations. The territory's capitalist system could continue to function as it had before 1997. Expatriates, except for those in the highest governmental positions, would be allowed to continue in their jobs. At least in the early years following the transfer, Hong Kong's governor would be nominated by local representative organizations and then appointed by Beijing. And the Chinese central government would not impose taxes in Hong Kong.[52]

Many of these points had been raised on previous occasions, but the statements of Ji Pengfei, who was intimately involved with developing policy on Hong Kong, represented the most comprehensive picture of post–1997 Hong Kong yet and offered useful insights into the issues being discussed in the "secret" negotiations.

In response to the British concession on administration, the Chinese attitude toward the talks took a favorable turn at this time as well. Vice–Foreign Minister Qian Qichen on November 1 explained that the September 1984 deadline for an agreement was not so strict after all, and that talks would go on until an acceptable solution had been reached.[53] On November 15, Ji Pengfei confirmed in a meeting with Hong Kong residents that China would guarantee Hong Kong's capitalist system and way of life for fifty years, a formula that was to become a centerpiece of the Sino-British pact. Ji called the PRC's claim to sovereignty "unquestionable and a fact that heaven and earth would only agree to." But he explained that under Article 31 of the PRC's constitution, Hong Kong people could rule Hong Kong and they could write specific freedoms into the territory's own laws.[54]

In a speech at Hong Kong University on January 10, 1984, Xu Jiatun, who had earlier replaced Wang Kuang as director of NCNA's Hong Kong branch, repeated the terms that Ji Pengfei had outlined to Denny Huang, adding that they "are formulated on the basis of respecting history and reality and taking into account the interests of all parties concerned in Hong Kong."[55] Other officials echoed Xu's speech in the following weeks, insisting on what he had called China's "unshakable position" on sovereignty, repeating the terms under which the SAR would function, and calling for an early resolution to the question. Having accused the British of playing the "opinion card," the Chinese were continuing their own United Front strategy to garner support for their plans.

But Hong Kong residents remained skeptical. In late February 1984, an unofficial (non–civil servant) member of Hong Kong's Legislative Council (Legco) introduced a motion to debate any proposals for Hong Kong's future agreed upon by the Chinese and British. Xu Jiatun's immediate response was cautious—he said only that the British authorities would handle the matter.[56] A few days later, the chairman of the Guangdong session of the CPPCC, Liang Weilin, reacted more strongly, stating that the Legislative Council "can debate anything . . . from the south sky to the north land. . . . But the Hong Kong issue is a matter between the Chinese and the British Governments."[57] When the motion was passed in March, NCNA criticized the event as Britain's renewed attempt to establish a "three-legged stool," but its criticism was limited.[58] By this time, the Chinese were confident that an agreement would be reached by the end of the summer, and they knew the British would not attempt to rewrite it in response to public opinion in Hong Kong.

Hong Kong residents were further troubled by Deng Xiaoping's announcement in April 1984 that PLA troops would be stationed in Hong Kong after 1997. To Deng, this was the clear prerogative of a sovereign power: "How can Hong Kong be described as Chinese territory if we don't have the right to station troops there?" he reportedly asked. But to the colony's residents it was an ominous reminder of their vulnerability. The announcement shocked Hong Kong's citizens and set off another tremor in its stock market. Later, Hong Kong residents accepted grudgingly the inevitability of seeing PLA troops in the territory, but the number of troops and their role in the SAR continued to be issues of great concern.

Concluding the Agreement

The negotiations had begun in 1984 with new players. Sir Richard Evans, the new ambassador to China, had replaced Sir Percy Cradock as head of the British team and Vice Foreign Minister Zhou Nan had replaced Yao Guang on the Chinese side. With the major issues of principle behind them, progress was brisk, and by August only three substantive areas remained: nationality, civil aviation and land.

Nationality in the Hong Kong SAR posed a sticky problem because of its relationship to sovereignty. About 3.25 million of Hong Kong's residents are recognized as British Dependent Territories Citizens (BDTC) and travel with British passports. The British wanted to permit them to retain that privilege after 1997. The Chinese, however, saw this as an infringement of their sovereignty and argued firmly against the idea. Through informal contacts, however, the Chinese negotiators informed the British that their real objection was against recognition of SAR residents as British nationals. They would be willing to allow those residents to use British passports for travel purposes alone.[59] This concession provided the foundation for an agreement on nationality and travel documents, the details of which would be worked out in the SAR's Basic Law.

In civil aviation, the British were concerned that Cathay Pacific, Hong Kong's major airline, would have its routes usurped by the Chinese flag carrier, CAAC. Recognizing the symbolic impact of any decision that pushed Cathay aside, the Chinese agreed to allow the airline to maintain its routes after 1997 and to permit the SAR government to negotiate for additional routes outside China.

Land posed another difficult problem. The British wanted Chinese consent to lease land in Hong Kong for periods ending after 1997, while the Chinese demanded a role in lease decisions. The Chinese also feared that the Hong Kong government, which earns substantial revenue from the annual sale of land leases, might sell off large chunks on the eve of the transfer, with the profits going to the departing British. To settle the issue, the Chinese proposed that some portion of land revenues be set aside in an account that would be held for the SAR government. The British agreed to this arrangement, with fifty percent of all land revenues to be set aside.[60]

With these three obstacles removed, the agreement was ready by mid-September. The two sides had agreed that it would be called a "Joint Declaration." This represented a compromise between British concerns that the agreement be legally binding and Chinese fears that signing a "treaty" would grant legitimacy to the unequal treaties by which Hong Kong was acquired. Ambassador Evans and Vice Foreign Minister Zhou initialled the document in Beijing on September 26, 1984.

China's Involvement in the Colony

Rapid expansion of the PRC's involvement in Hong Kong continued through the early 1980s as part of a deliberate policy to play a more active role in the colony's economy. Primarily through China Resources and the Bank of China Group, the PRC invested heavily in real estate, construction and various joint commercial ventures. Mainland-connected companies doing business in the colony continued to increase their operations, and trade delegations from Chinese provinces and cities visited Hong Kong to court joint-venture investments. Everbright Company, a private firm run by a mainland Chinese that was the first of its kind, was established in Hong Kong in August 1983 to serve as an agent for China's Ministry of Foreign Economic Relations and Trade and to introduce foreign businessmen to investment in China. The company announced in February 1984 that it had completed six deals worth US$48 million and planned to spend US$150 million on technology and equipment for China in the coming year, confirming its intention to become a major actor in Chinese trade with and through the colony.[61] Trade between Hong Kong and the mainland continued to expand, as did transportation and communications links. The initiation of direct air service between Hong Kong and the mainland in 1978 was followed in the early 1980s by additional agreements on train, ferry and telephone services. A joint-venture agreement to build a 240–kilometer highway linking Hong Kong, Guangzhou, and the two Special Economic Zones of Shenzhen and Zhuhai was signed in September 1984, further symbolizing Hong Kong's intimate ties with the mainland.

Taxi Strike

The Chinese government's claim to responsibility for Hong Kong residents has always been a delicate issue in Hong Kong politics. It reemerged in January 1984, when the Hong Kong government announced a plan to increase license fees, registration charges and fare rates for all taxis. Taxi drivers, who saw their incomes threatened by the scheme, were outraged and organized a large-scale strike that seriously disrupted traffic. At the end of the strike's second day, looters took advantage of the disruption to smash store windows and steal merchandise, sparking a riot. An estimated 10,000 people were involved in the rioting, 130 were charged with crimes, and damage amounted to almost US$600,000. Though observers were quick to point out that the rioting and looting had no direct link to the strikers' actions, the strike had created an atmosphere of heightened tension and disorder that was conducive to such behavior. The following morning Hong Kong was again quiet, and the drivers returned to work when two Legislative Councillors announced they would oppose the increases, which were later defeated.[62]

As in several previous disputes between workers and the Hong Kong government, the taxi drivers sought support for their case from the Chinese central government. Representatives of the taxi operators' unions took their complaints about the proposed increases to Hong Kong's NCNA office and requested a personal meeting with Xu Jiatun to discuss the issue. The Chinese government was reluctant to get involved in what it saw as Hong Kong's internal matter, however, particularly at a time when the colony's economy seemed so sensitive to every word from Beijing. Xu would not meet with the strikers, and his deputy, Qi Feng, offered only "sympathy" for their problems. "We have all along paid close attention to the matter. But the Xinhua [NCNA] Hong Kong branch is not the Hong Kong Government, and there is a special department in the Hong Kong Government which is responsible for handling the matter . . . we believe that the relevant department will with a view to maintaining Hong Kong's stability and prosperity take prompt measures to reasonably handle the matter." He told the drivers to "prevent the disturbance of unstable factors," and to work for "stability and prosperity." Wishing them success, Qi sent the disappointed strikers on their way.[63] The Chinese government in this case was even less willing than in the past to support the grievances of Hong Kong workers. No official statement about the riots was issued. In a visit to Canton two weeks later, Deng Xiaoping said he was "very pleased that the incidents had been amicably resolved."[64]

A less congenial response was given a group of villagers from Tin Shui Wan in the New Territories, who in April 1984 took their complaints over government compensation for their land directly to Beijing. Their public demonstration in the Chinese capital was broken up, and public security officers detained three demonstrators and one Hong Kong reporter who was recording the event.[65] This minor incident revealed an element of Chinese policy toward Hong Kong that was to cause serious concern among the colony's residents. Chinese officials were so committed to preserving the colony's economic stability that they appeared willing to sacrifice the colony's civil rights to do so.

China's Hong Kong Policy Under Pressure

The PRC's official stance on the Hong Kong question entered a crucial new phase beginning in the late 1970s. Its long-held position that Hong Kong was a question left over from history that would be resolved "when conditions are ripe" had become invalid, as conditions had ripened of their own accord. For the first time since the New Territories was leased, the Chinese government was forced to make an explicit commitment regarding its intentions toward the territory. Nevertheless, the new Chinese position that emerged in the early 1980s included important similarities with past Chinese policies.

The mainstay of the Chinese argument continued to be an insistence on sovereignty, as it had been since the 1920s. Premier Zhao Ziyang admitted that, given a choice between sovereignty over Hong Kong and the preservation of the economic benefits Hong Kong offered, the PRC would choose the former.[66] The question of sovereignty rekindled painful memories of humiliations suffered at the hands of imperialists and heroic memories of the struggle to regain China's national integrity. Regaining sovereignty over Hong Kong was, as one NCNA article phrased it, a "historical mission which cannot be obstructed by any force."[67]

A second fundamental aspect of the PRC's approach to the Hong Kong question was an insistence on the invalidity of the unequal treaties. International law decreed that unequal treaties were invalid, the Chinese government argued, and therefore there was no sense in debating the terms of the specific treaties that concerned Hong Kong, even if the British government considered them legitimate. The PRC therefore retained the right to take back Hong Kong whenever it wished.

Within the context of these broad principles, however, there was considerable room for maneuver. As long as the Chinese central government was granted sovereignty over Hong Kong, it was willing to accord the Hong Kong SAR a degree of autonomy well beyond that of any other Chinese subnational unit. And as long as the British did not insist on the validity of the treaties, the Chinese were willing to negotiate for their abrogation and to work for a smooth transfer of administration. Of course, sovereignty and the validity of the treaties were two issues on which Prime Minister Thatcher had taken a hard-line stance during her visit to Beijing in September 1982, a strategy for which she was strongly criticized in Beijing and London. In the negotiations that followed, however, the British conceded sovereignty and administration in Hong Kong to the PRC, and the Chinese responded by agreeing to specific guarantees that, if honored, would grant Hong Kong considerable autonomy.

Meanwhile, the Chinese continued to expand their own involvement in the colony and to contribute to Hong Kong's prosperity. In October 1982, for example, the Bank of China boasted that it had taken measures to help halt the Hong Kong dollar's precipitous decline and that it had negotiated a plan to offer, together with private banks, twenty-year mortgages in Hong Kong.[68] Beijing also hailed its contributions to the colony's survival, through the sale of food and other daily necessities at low prices, supplies which they continued to provide even when floods caused the suspension of train service. Such contributions were not crucial to Hong Kong's economic growth,[69] but by referring to them Chinese officials were attempting to prove that they had always placed a high value on Hong Kong's well-being.

Understanding Chinese Motives

The PRC's policy toward Hong Kong in this crucial period and its approach to negotiating an agreement on the colony's future appears to have been influenced by several factors, all of which had been present to some degree in the past. Unlike the Nationalists, the Communists were not preoccupied with more pressing foreign policy matters; rather, national reunification was at the top of the Beijing leadership's agenda of long-term goals. Nor were they constrained by insufficient military power to take the colony by force. In fact, it is in the context of Hong Kong's extreme vulnerability that Chinese policy appears particularly accommodative. The PRC could have taken Hong Kong back through unilateral action, beginning with the halting of supplies to the colony, at any time. Instead, it pursued reunification cautiously, with respect for the historical peculiarities of Hong Kong's position.

One reason for this approach was the PRC's continued desire to appear as a responsible actor in world affairs. Chinese officials recognized that PRC policy toward Hong Kong affected not only Hong Kong and British interests, but also American, Japanese, and numerous other countries' as well. They stressed on several occasions their desire to protect the investment climate in Hong Kong in order to continue to attract foreign capital, an important element of the colony's economy. In his January 1984 speech at Hong Kong University, for example, Xu Jiatun explained that Beijing's future plans for Hong Kong were designed to win international as well as domestic support.[70]

The Chinese leadership was also concerned that its deliberations on Hong Kong be well received in Taiwan. Taiwan was clearly the big piece in the reunification puzzle, and despite extreme skepticism in Taipei, leaders in Beijing hoped that a favorable resolution to the Hong Kong question would help convince Taiwan to accept the mainland's reunification proposals. An article in the December 1983 issue of *Beijing Review* discussed in detail the similarities and differences between the Hong Kong and Taiwan reunification issues and concluded that both should be established as Special Administrative Regions.[71] On separate occasions, both Deng Xiaoping and Zhao Ziyang suggested that the "one country, two systems" formula would be appropriate for Taiwan's reunification with the mainland.

The PRC's approach to resolving the Hong Kong question was also intended to retain the benefits that the colony had long provided to the mainland. As China's leaders looked to the West for technology and expertise to aid the Four Modernizations, Hong Kong continued to serve as a convenient point of access. Li Qiang in 1978 said that, "We will . . . send as many people to Hong Kong so that we can have as much contact, so we can make a positive contribution to the Four Modernizations of China."[72] The establishment of Everbright Company in Hong Kong confirmed the Chinese perception of the colony's environment as especially favorable to international trade. Not only did the company enjoy communications, transportation and other service advantages over its mainland counterparts, but Everbright Chairman Wang Guangying pointed out that in Hong Kong he was able to make deals with countries that did not have diplomatic relations with China.[73] And Xu Jiatun called Hong Kong "a bridge to transmit world economic information, to learn experience in enterprise management and to absorb funds, technologies and qualified personnel."[74]

Of course, Hong Kong provided substantial immediate economic benefits as well. Between 1976 and 1984, trade between Hong Kong and the mainland rose sharply, making Hong Kong the PRC's greatest entrepôt trade market and source of imports, and China the fourth largest export market for Hong Kong manufactured goods.[75] As the source of approximately one third of China's foreign exchange,[76] Hong Kong provided the funds China needed to buy foreign technology essential to its modernization program. The PRC earned that foreign exchange not only through trade, but also through its business operations, real estate holdings, financial institutions, investments and travel agency receipts in the territory. Hong Kong residents also sent gifts to their mainland relatives and made contributions to build roads, hospitals, schools and other social welfare projects, mostly in Guangdong. These factors combined to give China a large trade surplus with the colony.

There is no doubt that Chinese leaders worked deliberately to take advantage of the PRC's economic ties with Hong Kong, but the economic motivation alone may not be sufficient to explain Chinese behavior. Annual earnings from Hong Kong in the early 1980s amounted to less than one percent of China's gross national product, so that China could hardly be considered financially dependent on the colony. The loss of those earnings—particularly the crucial foreign exchange—would be seriously damaging, but the Chinese economy could be expected to recover from it.[77]

The various benefits Hong Kong provided to the mainland had to some degree been present for decades, but they took on new significance in this period, as a modernization program that relied on an "open door" coincided with the British request for resolution of the colony's status. The tension that had long existed between China's claim to sovereignty and its acquiescence to Hong Kong's status quo finally reached a climax. The PRC's resolution of that tension reflects its commitment to the principles of sovereignty and territorial integrity, as well as its recognition of the advantages that would continue to accrue to the mainland by maintaining Hong Kong's status quo. The agreement on Hong Kong's future was designed to satisfy both of these imperatives. Whether the agreement's promises can be carried out remains to be seen.

Notes

1. Foreign Broadcast Information Service (FBIS), *Daily Report: China*, Nov. 27, 1978, A14.

2. *South China Morning Post (Post)*, March 30, 1979, 1, in FBIS, Dec. 20, 1978, A26.

3. *New China News Agency (NCNA)*, March 10, 1980, in FBIS, March 14, 1980, E6.

4. *Post*, May 12, 1980, 1.

5. *Post*, March 30, 1979, 1.

6. Joseph Y. S. Cheng, ed., *Hong Kong in Transition* (Hong Kong: Oxford University Press, 1986): 67.

7. *Asia Yearbook, 1980* (Hong Kong: Far Eastern Economic Review): 160.

8. Joseph Y. S. Cheng, "The Future of Hong Kong: A Hong Kong Belonger's View," *International Affairs* 58 (Summer 1982): 486.

9. Cheng, "Future," 483.

10. *Beijing Review* 22, no. 41 (Oct. 12, 1979): 11.

11. *NCNA*, Oct. 7, 1980.

12. *Post*, Nov. 15, 1980, 1, in FBIS, Nov. 17, 1980, E6–7.

13. *Beijing Review* 24, no. 15 (April 13, 1981): 8.

14. *NCNA*, July 18, 1981, in FBIS, July 22, 1981, E5.

15. *NCNA*, Oct. 8, 1987, in FBIS, Oct. 9, 1987, 35; David Bonavia, *Hong Kong 1997* (Hong Kong: South China Morning Post, 1983): 77.

16. Y. C. Jao, "Hong Kong's Role in Financing China's Modernization," in A. J. Youngson, ed., *China and Hong Kong: The Economic Nexus* (Hong Kong: Oxford University Press, 1983): 31.

17. Nai Ruenn Chen, "China's Foreign Trade in Global Perspective," in James C. Hsiung and Samuel S. Kim, eds., *China in the Global Community* (N.Y.: Praeger Publishers, 1980): 135.

18. *Hong Kong 1983* (Hong Kong: Government Printer, 1983): 2.

19. Norman Miners, "Can the Colony of Hong Kong Survive 1997?," *Asia Pacific Community* 6 (Fall 1979): 102.

20. Robert Delfs, "1997 and All That," *Far Eastern Economic Review (FEER)* 117, no. 29 (July 16–22, 1982): 15–16.

21. *NCNA*, July 16, 1982, in FBIS, July 19, 1982, K3–4.

22. Cited in *Summary of World Broadcasts Part 3: The Far East*, July 13, 1980, 1–2.

23. *Post*, August 3, 1982, 1.

24. *Hong Kong Standard*, August 11, 1982.

25. *AFP*, August 23, 1982, in FBIS, August 26, 1982, E1.

26. *NCNA*, Sept. 22, 1982, in FBIS, Sept. 23, 1982, G2.

27. *NCNA*, Sept. 30, 1982, in FBIS, Oct. 1, 1982, E1.

28. *NCNA*, Sept. 30, 1982, in FBIS, Oct. 1, 1982, E1.

29. *AFP*, Oct. 7, 1982, in FBIS, Oct. 8, 1982, E1; *Post*, Dec. 26, 1983, 8.

30. *Post*, Dec. 26, 1983, 8.

31. *Asian Wall Street Journal*, Nov. 1, 1982.

32. *Post*, Dec. 26, 1983, 8.

33. *Post*, May 18, 1983, in FBIS, May 18, 1983, W3–4; Frank Ching, *Hong Kong and China: For Better or For Worse* (N.Y.: Foreign Policy Association, 1985): 13–15.

34. *Post*, Dec. 26, 1983, 8.

35. *Post*, Dec. 26, 1983, 8.

36. *China News Agency*, June 25, 1983, in FBIS, June 27, 1983, E1; *NCNA*, June 25, 1983, in FBIS, July 6, 1983, E1.

37. *AFP*, June 27, 1983, in FBIS, June 28, 1983, E1.

38. *AFP*, July 7, 1983, in FBIS, July 8, 1983, E1.

39. *Post*, Dec. 26, 1983, 9.

40. Quoted in Bonavia, *Hong Kong*, 100–1.

41. *Post*, Dec. 26, 1983, 9.

42. *Post*, Dec. 26, 1983, 9.

43. *Asia Yearbook, 1983*, 146.

44. *Ching Pao*, Sept. 1982, in *Tongxiang 1997: Xianggang Qiantu Wenti Zhuanji* [*Onward to 1997: Special Edition on the Question of Hong Kong's Future*] (Hong Kong: Mirror Cultural Enterprises, Ltd., 1983): 12; *People's Daily*, Sept. 20, 1983, in FBIS, Sept. 21, 1983, E1–6.

45. *NCNA*, Sept. 21, 1983, in FBIS, Sept. 22, 1983, E1.

46. *NCNA*, Sept. 15, 1983, in FBIS, Sept. 16, 1983, E1.

47. *NCNA*, Sept. 19, 1983, in FBIS, Sept. 20, 1983, E2.

48. *Post*, Oct. 1, 1983, 1.

49. See *Post*, Sept. 22, 1983, 1; Oct 5, 1983, 4; Oct. 16, 1983, 10.

50. *Post*, Oct. 16, 1983, 10.

51. *Post*, Sept. 30, 1983, 1.

52. *Post*, Oct. 15, 1983, 1.

53. *Post*, Nov. 3, 1983, 1.

54. *Post*, Nov. 16, 1983, 1. Xu Dixin, a member of the NPC Standing Committee, had referred to the fifty-year pledge in September.

55. *NCNA*, Jan. 10, 1984, in FBIS, Jan. 11, 1984, E2.

56. *Post*, Feb. 25, 1984, 8.

57. *NCNA*, March 1, 1984 in FBIS, March 2, 1984, E1.

58. Ching, *Hong Kong*, 29.

59. *Kuang Chiao Ching* [Wide Angle] 145 (Oct. 16, 1984): 8–11, in FBIS, Oct. 29, 1984, W1–7; Ching, *Hong Kong*, 30.

60. *Post*, March 15, 1984, 1.

61. *Post*, Feb. 27, 1984, B1.

62. Theresa Ma, "A Taximan Standoff," *FEER* 123, no. 4 (Jan. 26, 1984): 17–18.

63. *NCNA*, Jan. 13, 1984, in FBIS, Jan. 13, 1984, E3.

64. *Post*, Feb. 23, 1984, 10.

65. Charles F. Emmons, "Public Opinion and Participation in Pre–1997 Hong Kong," in Y.C. Jao, et al., eds., *Hong Kong and 1997: Strategies for the Future* (Hong Kong: Centre of Asian Studies, University of Hong Kong, 1985): 65.

66. *Post*, Oct. 24, 1983, 15.

67. *China News Agency*, Jan. 28, 1983, in FBIS, Feb. 4, 1983, E2.

68. *AFP*, Oct. 6, 1982, in FBIS, Oct. 9, 1982, E1.

69. See L. C. Chau, "Imports of Consumer Goods from China and the Economic Growth of Hong Kong," in Youngson, ed., *China and Hong Kong*, 184–225.

70. *NCNA*, Jan. 10, 1984, in FBIS, Jan. 11, 1984, E2.

71. *Beijing Review*, no. 52 (Dec. 26, 1983): 4, in FBIS, Jan. 5, 1984, E1–3.

72. *Post*, Dec. 20, 1978, in FBIS, Dec. 20, 1978, A27.

73. *NCNA*, Aug. 18, 1983, in FBIS, Aug. 19, 1983, E1.

74. *Wen Wei Po*, Nov. 7, 1984, in FBIS, Nov. 8, 1984, W1–2.

75. *People's Daily*, Feb. 12, 1984, in FBIS, Feb. 16, 1984, E3.

76. Various estimates of China's foreign exchange earnings from Hong Kong have been offered, ranging from twenty-five to forty percent. A Chinese research organization estimated thirty-one percent. See the article by Frank Ching in *Asian Wall Street Journal*, Feb. 18, 1983.

77. See Jao, "Hong Kong's Role," in Youngson, ed., *China and Hong Kong*, 60.

6

One Country, Two Systems: An Agreement on Hong Kong's Future

On December 19, 1984, British Prime Minister Margaret Thatcher and Chinese Premier Zhao Ziyang signed the Joint Declaration that would end a century and a half of British rule in Hong Kong. After approval by the British Parliament and the Chinese National People's Congress, instruments of ratification were exchanged in June 1984. In the long history of the Hong Kong question, this agreement represented both an end and a beginning. It resolved the long-standing question of Hong Kong's status by detailing the terms under which the territory would return to Chinese sovereignty. At the same time, the agreement initiated a crucial new phase in Hong Kong's history. In the years leading up to 1997, the political structure of the Hong Kong Special Administrative Region and the relationship between the SAR and the Chinese central government will take shape. The result of that process will determine the future of Hong Kong and its 5.6 million residents.

The Sino-British Agreement

The agreement signed in Beijing consists of a "Joint Declaration on the Question of Hong Kong" and three annexes. The Joint Declaration summarizes Chinese and British plans for the return of Hong Kong to Chinese sovereignty as a Special Administrative Region. The first annex details Chinese plans for maintaining the territory's status quo, the second describes plans for the formation of a "Joint Liaison Group," consisting of five representatives from each side, to monitor implementation of the Joint Declaration, and the third describes a Sino-British agreement for resolution of the thorny problem of land leases. Finally, two memoranda from the Chinese and British governments discuss the issues of nationality and travel documents after 1997.

The Joint Declaration's status as a bilateral agreement reflects Beijing's sensitivity to the legacy of unequal treaties. The British had hoped to sign a formal treaty, but the Chinese rejected that proposal on the grounds that the treaties by which Great Britain had acquired Hong Kong were invalid, and therefore the Hong Kong issue was a domestic matter that the PRC was entitled to resolve on its own. A "joint declaration" was merely a statement of Great Britain's and the PRC's intention to cooperate in returning the territory to China. Nevertheless, the Chinese side agreed that the Joint Declaration would be registered along with other treaties at the United Nations, and several mainland legal experts insisted publicly that the agreement was legally binding.

The contents of the Joint Declaration were no surprise to those who had followed the course of the "secret" talks in Beijing. The pillars on which it rested were the Chinese intentions to recover full sovereignty over the territory and to preserve the status quo. This would be accomplished through the "one country, two systems" and "Hong Kong people ruling Hong Kong" formulas that the Chinese had proposed during the negotiations, and that the establishment of the SAR was designed to facilitate.

Details of the Agreement

The Joint Declaration echoes familiar themes from the history of Chinese policy toward Hong Kong. Without mentioning the three "unequal" treaties that ceded and leased Hong Kong to the British, it describes the Hong Kong problem as a question "left over from history," the settlement of which "is conducive to the maintenance of the prosperity and stability of Hong Kong and to the further strengthening and development of the relations between the two countries on a new basis." Hong Kong's return to the mainland is called "the common aspiration of the entire Chinese people," and necessary to "upholding national unity and territorial integrity."

The document then presents a twelve-point list of intentions that constitutes the heart of the agreement and the center of PRC policy after 1997. ". . . taking account of the history of Hong Kong and its realities, the People's Republic of China has decided to establish, in accordance with the provisions of Article 31 of the Constitution of the People's Republic of China, a Hong Kong Special Administrative Region upon resuming the exercise of sovereignty over Hong Kong." While under the authority of the central government, according to the Joint Declaration, Hong Kong will enjoy a substantial degree of autonomy, including its own executive, legislative and judicial powers. In order to realize the concept of "Hong Kong people ruling Hong Kong," the government will be composed of local residents, and foreign nationals may hold certain posts. Social and economic systems will not be changed, nor will Hong Kong's status as a free port and separate customs territory. There will be a free flow of capital and the Hong Kong dollar will remain freely convertible. The SAR's finances will be independent of Beijing, and the territory may enter independently into international agreements. Hong Kong will issue its own travel documents. Maintenance of public order will be the responsibility of the SAR government. Finally, all of these elements are to be codified in a Basic Law of the Hong Kong SAR, and are to remain unchanged for fifty years.

The Joint Declaration's first annex spells out in greater detail the Chinese promises of autonomy and fifty years of an unchanged capitalist system. This section is a tribute to British negotiators, who insisted over Chinese objections that the Joint Declaration include specific guarantees. Reserving for the central government the areas of defense and foreign affairs, the document reiterates that the SAR shall have executive, legislative and judicial power, including power of final adjudication. The SAR's chief executive will be chosen "by election or through consultations held locally," then appointed by the National People's Congress. Other top officials will be nominated by the SAR's chief executive and formally appointed by the NPC. The legislature will be returned by elections. The English language may be used in the government and in the courts, and Hong Kong may fly its own regional flag alongside the Chinese national flag. Hong Kong's laws will remain basically unchanged, and the SAR legislature will have power to pass new laws or alter existing ones. There will be no interference in Hong Kong's independent judicial power, and court decisions may refer to precedents from other common law jurisdictions. Judges will be appointed by the SAR chief executive. Hong Kong government employees of any nationality may continue in their jobs after 1997 and will be entitled to normal benefits and pensions.

The first annex promises financial autonomy for Hong Kong, an issue that PRC negotiators recognized to be crucial to the territory's continued prosperity. The SAR government will establish its own internal taxation system and will not be obligated to submit taxes to the central government. Property will continue to be protected by law, and the SAR will maintain "the capitalist economic and trade systems previously practiced in Hong Kong." The SAR may establish its own trade missions in foreign countries. It will remain an international financial center, retaining its existing markets for foreign exchange, gold, securities and futures. The SAR will issue its own currency, and after 1997 will gradually replace "currency bearing references inappropriate to the status of Hong Kong as a Special Administrative Region of the People's Republic of China." Indeed, various references to Hong Kong's colonial status can be expected to disappear after 1997.

In recognition of Hong Kong's role as a major shipping center, the first annex promises that the SAR will be authorized to maintain its own shipping register and issue related documents under the name, "Hong Kong, China." Access to the SAR's ports will be determined by the SAR government, except in the case of foreign warships. Hong Kong will also maintain its own aircraft register, and the SAR government will be responsible for the management of civil aviation.

Hong Kong's education system will not be changed. Private schools, including those with religious affiliation, will be allowed to continue to operate, and students will have the same freedom of choice, including the pursuit of education overseas. Some curriculum changes, including an increased focus on the PRC and learning Mandarin, were already apparent by the mid-1980s and will become more prominent after 1997, but the Chinese government claims that it will not mandate such changes.

Hong Kong will retain limited autonomy in its foreign affairs. Under the name, "Hong Kong, China," it may participate in PRC delegations to international conferences and organizations and may negotiate on its own certain agreements, particularly regarding trade, with foreign governments. International agreements to which the PRC is not a party may remain in force in Hong Kong. The status of foreign missions in Hong Kong will be extended or altered based on each government's relations with the PRC. The Sino-British agreement confirms that PLA troops will be stationed in Hong Kong but promises that they will not be allowed to interfere in the SAR's internal affairs. Hong Kong will not be responsible for the cost of maintaining its PLA garrison (the colony currently shares the bill for Britain's Hong Kong garrison with London).

The first annex to the Joint Declaration promises to maintain the existing rights and freedoms of Hong Kong residents, including those relating to speech, the press, assembly, association, correspondence, travel, trade unions, strikes and demonstrations, choice of occupation, academic research, marriage, and the family. Religious organizations and their affiliated institutions will be allowed to operate as before. Furthermore, the International Covenant on Civil and Political Rights and the International Covenant on Economic, Social and Cultural Rights will remain in force in Hong Kong. Most Hong Kong residents view such rights and freedoms as central to their continued way of life and were pleased to see them listed explicitly, yet they fear that the Joint Declaration's guarantees in this regard may not be reliable.

The Hong Kong SAR will issue its own resident identity cards to those who qualify, including any persons (and the children of those persons) who have continuously resided in Hong Kong for a minimum of seven years before or after 1997, including non-Chinese nationals who claim Hong Kong as their place of permanent residence and any other persons who had the right of abode only in Hong Kong prior to establishment of the SAR. Those persons will be issued travel documents by the SAR and will be free to leave Hong Kong without special authorization. Regulation of entry into Hong Kong from China will remain essentially unchanged, in order to prevent an influx of PRC residents hoping to enjoy the SAR's high standard of living.

Annex Two of the Joint Declaration establishes a Joint Liaison Group (JLG) to facilitate communication between the two sides during the transition period and to discuss issues relevant to the transition. Scheduled to be disbanded in 2000, the JLG has no formal administrative or supervisory powers. However, since 1985 the JLG has met regularly to discuss the most sensitive and pressing issues of the Sino-British agreement, including travel agreements, participation in international organizations, adherence to international conventions and nationality. In addition to its formal role, the JLG has served as a forum for mainland officials to gain a better understanding of how Hong Kong functions and what types of policies will be required (or must be avoided) for it to continue to prosper. Frequent informal contacts between PRC and Hong Kong officials have served a similar purpose.

Annex Three of the Joint Declaration deals specifically with land leases, the issue that originally led the British to raise the Hong Kong question with the Beijing government. This part of the document grants legal status to all leases that extend beyond June 30, 1997, and allows leases to be granted for periods extending through June 30, 2047. It also limits the total amount of new land leased by the Hong Kong government to fifty hectares per year, to prevent the government from disposing of its land holdings in order to make a windfall profit. (The limit was exceeded in 1988, however, at the request of the Hong Kong government and after consultation between the Chinese and British sides.) Net income from government land sales is to be placed in a Capital Works Reserve Fund and shared between the current Hong Kong government and the future SAR government, for use in land development and public works projects. Finally, the third annex establishes a Land Commission comprised of members from the Chinese and British sides. Scheduled to be dissolved in 1997, the Land Commission has met regularly to discuss land sales, proposals for public works projects and other related issues.

In addition to the three annexes, the Sino-British agreement includes an exchange of memoranda on the issue of nationality, which the Chinese found too sensitive to include in the main text of the Joint Declaration.

The British memorandum explains that Hong Kong residents registered previously as British Dependent Territories Citizens (BDTCs) will lose their BDTC status, but will be issued passports by the British government. (BDTC passports were replaced by British Nationality Overseas [BNO] passports beginning in July 1987.) The Chinese memorandum responds by stating that all Hong Kong Chinese compatriots are Chinese nationals, whether they hold a BDTC passport or not. Nevertheless, "taking account of the historical background of Hong Kong and its realities," the government of the PRC will allow Hong Kong residents previously holding BDTC status to use travel documents issued by Great Britain.

A Diplomatic Success

The Sino-British agreement in many respects is a remarkable document. Once the issue of formal sovereignty was conceded, PRC negotiators granted substantive, specific concessions that were intended to preserve Hong Kong's status quo. The amount of autonomy granted to the SAR is unprecedented; the freedom to negotiate international agreements independently and to use travel documents issued by a foreign government, for example, are most unusual. Beijing's promise to maintain Hong Kong's social and economic systems for a period of fifty years is also an unusual step that was clearly designed to ease fears in the colony. The fifty-year time period itself is not especially meaningful—Deng Xiaoping later indicated that Hong Kong's way of life might continue for 100 years or more—but it makes the Chinese promise to maintain the status quo sound more concrete and allows time for the standard of living in the mainland to approach Hong Kong's, as Chinese leaders have argued it will.

The agreement was a victory for both the Chinese and British sides. For the Chinese, it represented a sophisticated and subtle compromise between the inviolable principle of sovereignty and the practical question of Hong Kong's unusual status. If implemented successfully, the agreement will return Hong Kong to the mainland, thereby satisfying the imperative of national reunification, but allow Hong Kong to function much as it has in the past, thereby preserving the numerous benefits it provides the PRC.

For the British, the agreement's achievements were less grand. Having conceded the central issues of sovereignty and administration, the most that British negotiators could fight for were specific promises regarding the territory's autonomy. The Joint Declaration is a testimony to their success in that regard, though on most issues the British negotiators were not in a position to impose major changes. Ultimately it was Chinese intentions toward the territory, the basic elements of which were formed before the negotiations began in earnest, that determined the shape of the final agreement.

In Hong Kong, the draft agreement was warmly received when it was made public in September 1984. The document's provisions for Hong Kong's autonomy were broader than many had expected. The stock market, reflecting the colony's collective mood, responded favorably. Still, certain aspects of the agreement were unsettling to Hong Kong residents. The Joint Declaration promised autonomy, but how much autonomy? Would the Hong Kong SAR be permitted to make its own laws and not be overruled by the National People's Congress? Which of the PRC's laws would apply in Hong Kong? The division of legal authority was less clear than many would have liked, creating an impression that Beijing could easily impose its will in the SAR while complying formally with the Sino-British agreement. Similarly, the central government's role in selecting Hong Kong's chief executive was not spelled out in detail. Since Beijing retained the formal right to appoint Hong Kong's "governor" after 1997, how likely was it to exercise its veto power to insure that the chief executive was friendly to Beijing? As for the stationing of PLA troops in the SAR, it was not clear from the Joint Declaration whether they could be prevented from interfering in police and security matters.

Similar ambiguities surrounded the important issue of nationality. The agreement resolved the troublesome diplomatic issue of travel documents, but it failed to describe adequately the future status of holders of foreign passports. For example, would a Hong Kong Chinese with British nationality be allowed to serve in high leadership posts in the Hong Kong government? The status of Hong Kong's many non-Chinese residents, including Indians, Pakistanis and Southeast Asians who were born and raised in Hong Kong, also was not spelled out in the document. These people feared they might become stateless after 1997. And Hong Kong residents with BDTC or BNO status were not satisfied with the promise of British travel documents. They continued to hope for, and later would lobby actively for, a change in British policy that would grant them right of abode in Great Britain as insurance against a possible future crisis in Hong Kong.

Regarding the crucial area of the SAR's political structure, the Joint Declaration had little to say. Hong Kong's government and legislature would be composed of local residents chosen through elections or consultations. But details of these arrangements, including the time frame for the transition to an elected legislature, the nature of the electoral system and the role of political parties, were not explained. These issues would be left to discussions in the JLG and to the Basic Law drafting process, where they would generate considerable debate and controversy.

These specific concerns contributed to a general anxiety about the future that had already permeated Hong Kong society. Many of the colony's residents are refugees or family members of refugees from the mainland who have unhappy memories of life under the Communists and want nothing less than to be placed again under Beijing's rule. Even those who have no specific reason to fear the PRC are unwilling to submit to a future that is, if nothing else, uncertain. No agreement, no matter how conciliatory on the part of the Chinese government, can easily dispel such misgivings. Thus, while the Joint Declaration quelled many fears in Hong Kong, important questions remained unresolved. Having produced an agreement that was widely praised as a diplomatic success, PRC officials next faced the arduous tasks of drafting the SAR's Basic Law and convincing Hong Kong's residents of their intention to implement the Joint Declaration as written.

An End and a Beginning

The Sino-British agreement resolved the long-standing issue of Hong Kong's status in a manner that was in several important respects consistent with Chinese policy since the 1920s. But the agreement was more than a mere extension of China's existing Hong Kong policy; it was a novel solution to an unusual problem of domestic and foreign politics. Recognizing this, PRC officials have conceded publicly that implementation of the "one country, two systems" model they have developed will pose substantive challenges.

The agreement also set in motion a thirteen-year process of transition unlike any in the history of decolonization.[1] Though Britain had returned land to territorial sovereigns in the past, including the Chinese territory of Weihaiwei, it had never returned such an economically developed colony. This lack of precedent, compounded by the sensitivity of Hong Kong's stock market and the high international profile of the 1997 question, required that the Chinese and British move delicately as they formulated the rules and institutions that would facilitate implementation of the Joint Declaration.

Both signatories to the agreement hoped to guarantee a smooth transition of sovereignty, but both also had incentives for seeking to influence the shape of post–1997 Hong Kong government and society. Thus, while British and Chinese officials spoke publicly of their mutual commitment to cooperate in the transition process, they also were competing to influence the transition in different ways. The British were anxious to leave their mark on Hong Kong's political structure by putting in place some of the democratic mechanisms they had long denied the colony's residents, yet they recognized that the PRC had ultimate power to veto any changes after 1997. Chinese leaders had their own less democratic notions of how Hong Kong's government should be structured, but feared that overly aggressive attempts to impose their views would lead to economic and social instability in Hong Kong. The tension created by these competing forces became apparent as soon as the Sino-British agreement was signed.

Two tasks dominate Hong Kong's political landscape in the period leading up to July 1997. One is the drafting of the SAR's Basic Law, which will codify the promises made in the Joint Declaration. A second, related task is the determination and implementation of a new political structure that will be used to govern Hong Kong in the remaining years of British rule and in the SAR. For Britain and the PRC, successful completion of these two tasks will solidify the steps taken in the Joint Declaration toward the establishment of a viable SAR. For Hong Kong's residents, the stakes are much higher, since the Basic Law and the political structure of the SAR will determine the amount of true autonomy Hong Kong will enjoy after 1997, and therefore will profoundly affect their lives.

Drafting the Basic Law

The SAR's Basic Law promises to resolve many of the questions left unanswered in the Joint Declaration while creating the legal structure that will preserve China's sovereignty and Hong Kong's autonomy after 1997. The Basic Law drafting process has forced the Chinese to take firm positions on a number of difficult issues regarding Hong Kong's post–1997 administration. The Chinese have repeatedly confirmed their commitment to the principles expressed in the Joint Declaration, but they have occasionally been reluctant to accept what autonomy means in real terms, particularly as it relates to reform of the territory's political structure. This is a troubling problem, especially as Hong Kong's internal politics become more competitive and demands for democracy grow louder. If the "one country, two systems" and "Hong Kong people ruling Hong Kong" formulas are to work as the Chinese propose, the central government will have to act with considerable flexibility and restraint in the years ahead.

The Basic Law Drafting and Consultative Committees

After the signing of the Sino-British agreement, the issue of establishing a constitution and determining the political structure of the post–1997 SAR became urgent. Britain and the PRC both were anxious that these matters be settled well before 1997 to allow adequate time for the transition process and to promote confidence in Hong Kong's future stability. With this in mind, the Chinese central government in May 1985 established the Basic Law Drafting Committee (BLDC), charged with the complicated task of drafting the SAR's constitution.[2] The BLDC has five subcommittees devoted to major areas of discussion: the relationship between the Chinese central government and the SAR; the political system; the economy; rights and duties of Hong Kong SAR residents; and education, science, technology, culture, sports and religion. Of the fifty-nine members appointed, twenty-three were prominent Hong Kong residents, the others mainland Chinese. One mainland member died in 1986 and one Hong Kong member died in 1988, reducing the membership to fifty-seven. The Chinese membership of the BLDC includes several officials who were involved in making policy toward Hong Kong or participated in the Sino-British negotiations. Ji Pengfei, director of the State Council's Hong Kong and Macau Affairs Office, is its chairman. Working with him are several officials from the State Council's and the Foreign Ministry's respective Hong Kong and Macau Affairs Offices, representatives from NCNA (including Xu Jiatun), and other prominent political and academic figures. The selection of these high-level members reflects the significance the Chinese government attaches to the Hong Kong issue and its desire to maintain continuity in its policy.

Since the notion of a "mini-constitution" for Hong Kong was first raised during the Sino-British negotiations, PRC officials have insisted that its drafting is a matter for the Chinese government alone. The Chinese were fearful then, as later during the drafting process, of British attempts to influence the SAR's political structure, and of Hong Kong liberals who might lobby for radical political reforms. Chinese officials first indicated that the Basic Law would be drafted entirely in Beijing, but they later conceded that Hong Kong residents would at least be consulted before it was promulgated. Apparently in deference to concerns in Hong Kong, the Chinese finally agreed that Hong Kong residents could participate in the drafting process itself, though the participants were selected by the central government and were outnumbered by mainland members. Most of the Hong Kong delegates are prominent persons in industry and the professions, including several pro-Communist figures well known to Beijing, several wealthy conservatives and one prominent liberal, Martin Lee, who had earlier gained Beijing's respect but, together with fellow liberal Szeto Wah, turned out to be its most outspoken critic during the drafting process.

The BLDC held its first meeting in June 1985. Its schedule called for the completion of a first draft to be made available for public "consultation" in Hong Kong. A second series of drafting sessions would take public reaction into account and prepare another draft, which also would be presented for consultation. After the second period of consultation, the BLDC would draft a final version of the Basic Law and submit it to the National People's Congress for approval (pro forma) in 1990.

In order to facilitate the input of Hong Kong residents, the Chinese central government also established a Basic Law Consultative Committee (BLCC) composed of 180 members, all from Hong Kong. The BLCC's ostensible purpose was to collect and analyze opinions on the Basic Law drafts from all segments of Hong Kong society. Its efforts were hindered, however, by the failure of Chinese officials to communicate effectively just how the BLCC was expected to collect opinions and how the BLCC's conclusions were to be integrated into the Drafting Committee's work. Furthermore, although Beijing originally claimed that the BLCC would have equal status with the BLDC, the job of creating the committee was assigned to Hong Kong members of the BLDC. It was apparent even before its first meeting in December 1985 that the Consultative Committee in practice would be subordinate to the Drafting Committee, and that its influence would be strictly circumscribed.

The establishment of the BLCC was further marred by dispute in Hong Kong and clumsiness on the PRC's part.[3] One conflict broke out just prior to the December 1985 inauguration of the BLCC, when a Hong Kong labor leader was asked by pro-Communist labor leaders to withdraw his nomination to the committee. This move suggested that Beijing was anxious to keep BLCC members from attempting to influence the drafting process. A more serious dispute erupted in the first week of December, after the newly-appointed members of the BLCC, according to the rules of the committee's constitution, elected a nineteen-member Standing Committee. The rules called for the Standing Committee then to elect seven officers. Immediately following the election of the Standing Committee, however, leading members of the BLDC proposed their own slate of seven officers, which the Standing Committee, apparently without giving thoughtful consideration to Committee rules, quickly approved. When these events were immediately criticized as demonstrating blatant disregard for the BLCC constitution, Xu Jiatun explained that the "consultation" undertaken by Standing Committee members could also be considered a form of "election," making its result legitimate.

At a BLCC Standing Committee meeting a week later, members agreed that proper procedure had not been followed and held a new election. Several members refused to accept nomination, however, and the original seven officers were reelected. The result was generally viewed in Hong Kong as a concession to Beijing's grip on the Basic Law drafting and consultation processes, as well as a troubling example of the Chinese side's willingness to disregard existing rules and procedures in order to achieve a desired outcome.

The First Draft

The Basic Law's first draft was made public on April 28, 1988. In many respects its contents reiterate and expand on the Joint Declaration. Referring to Article 31 of the Chinese Constitution and the principle of "one country, two systems," the document promises that, apart from foreign affairs and defense matters, the Hong Kong SAR will enjoy substantial autonomy, including legislative power and power of final adjudication. SAR residents will be entitled to the same freedoms and rights as are now guaranteed in Hong Kong, including freedom of speech, the press and association.

The Basic Law describes a post–1997 SAR political structure that looks very similar to the current arrangement, with the chief difference being the method by which top officials are to be selected. The chief executive will be chosen by election or "through consultations," then formally appointed by Beijing, and members of the Legislative Council will be selected through a combination of direct and indirect elections. The Basic Law details the functions and duties of the SAR's officials and lists grounds for their impeachment. It promises to maintain the existing judiciary system, with the addition of a Court of Final Appeal. The Basic Law provides more detail on the Joint Declaration's promises of fiscal autonomy, freedom to make external trade agreements, independent civil aviation and shipping provisions, autonomy in educational matters, and religious freedom.

From China's perspective, the draft Basic Law is an extremely conciliatory document which provides unprecedented assurances of autonomy that are designed to preserve Hong Kong's economic health. As in the case of the Joint Declaration, however, promises of autonomy come second in priority to the assertion of sovereignty over Hong Kong. And it was this tension between the principle of sovereignty and the practical requisites of autonomy that raised concerns among Hong Kong residents when the first draft was made public.

The relationship between Beijing and Hong Kong, in particular the manner in which decision-making power will be shared, is at the heart of the Basic Law. The Chinese central government has retained crucial powers in some aspects of the relationship and has left others ambiguous. For example, Beijing has retained the right to appoint the SAR's chief executive after he or she has been chosen locally and the right to appoint other top officials on the chief executive's recommendation. It is not clear from the document whether the appointments will be strictly a rubber stamp or will tempt leaders in Beijing to meddle in Hong Kong affairs by insisting on either an ideologically acceptable "leftist" candidate or a "conservative" candidate more likely to maintain the territory's established fiscal policies. Reports from one BLDC meeting indicated that the central government's appointments would be "substantive" rather than pro forma.[4] An additional requirement in the first draft that the chief executive "be accountable to the Central People's Government and the Hong Kong Special Administrative Region" raised concerns that he or she will be closely monitored by Beijing.

Article 16 of the first draft requires that laws enacted by Hong Kong's Legislative Council be reported to the NPC Standing Committee and gives the Standing Committee the right to revoke any law it deems "not in conformity with this law or legal procedures." Article 17 gives the Chinese State Council the right to impose laws relating to defense and foreign affairs on the SAR. Article 22 requires the SAR government to "prohibit by law any act designed to undermine national unity or subvert the Central People's Government," a sweeping statement that, if "national unity" were broadly defined, could be used to curtail the SAR's autonomy and deny its citizens civil rights. Two of the first draft's most troubling provisions from the perspective of Hong Kong residents appear near the end of the document. Article 169 stipulates, "The power of interpretation of this Law is vested in the Standing Committee of the National People's Congress." Article 170 gives to the NPC the additional power to amend the Basic Law.

That the Chinese should retain ultimate decision-making power over Hong Kong in certain areas, including defense, foreign affairs, appointment of top officials, and interpretation and amendment of the Basic Law—what Beijing sees as essential elements of sovereignty—is not surprising. From the PRC's perspective, "one country, two systems," is still *one* country. The Chinese consider their willingness to sign an international agreement on Hong Kong's future to represent a significant concession to Hong Kong's unusual status, and they have taken pains to remind British officials and Hong Kong residents that the Hong Kong question is, in the final analysis, a domestic one for China. A *People's Daily* article by the noted Chinese scholar Huan Xiang, for example, pointed out that "one country, two systems," is not "two sovereign states within one country," nor is it "two competing political entities within one country."[5] PRC drafters revealed similar sensitivities when some Hong Kong drafters suggested that the Basic Law grant all "residual powers" to the SAR. The Chinese side maintained that such a provision would constitute an infringement on the central government's sovereign powers. According to the Chinese view, Hong Kong is not to be an independent entity incorporated into a federal system, but an administrative region subordinate to the central government.[6]

Mainland Basic Law drafters have responded to concern over these issues by offering assurances that there will be no arbitrary interference in the SAR's affairs. Article 170, for example, says that the Committee for the Basic Law, to consist of equal numbers of mainland and Hong Kong members, will be permitted to submit its opinions on proposed amendments, and no amendment to the Basic Law "shall contravene the established basic policies of the People's Republic of China regarding Hong Kong," which are specified in the Joint Declaration.

Of course, even this statement is subject to the central government's own interpretation and therefore can hardly assuage fears in Hong Kong. The challenge for the PRC in drafting the Basic Law has been to make the promise of autonomy credible while making the principle of sovereignty real. The first draft of the Basic Law revealed the contradictions inherent in those two goals and, judging by the skepticism with which the draft was received, left the challenge unmet.

The Response in Hong Kong

Once the first draft was made public, the five-month process of consultation began. The response from the majority of Hong Kong residents was disappointing. While the PRC press applauded the input of Hong Kong residents, surveys within the colony revealed that few Hong Kong residents had read the draft and fewer still had taken the trouble to comment on it. When the consultation period ended on September 30, 1988, only about 2000 individual submissions had been received.[7] Such inattention among the broad masses of the colony's residents in part reflected the length and complexity of the document, but it also revealed the apathy of a populace that had long been excluded from political decision-making and doubted that individual opinions could have a measurable impact on Chinese policy.

Hong Kong's elites were far more vocal. Criticism of the Basic Law from individuals and professional associations was plentiful, and it focused on the division of power between the central government and the SAR. In an unusual move, even Governor Sir David Wilson criticized the Basic Law's stipulation that the SAR maintain low taxes and a balanced budget, arguing that such provisions would unnecessarily restrict the policy options of future leaders. Hong Kong legal associations expressed concern over inadequate provisions for autonomy and legal jurisdiction, questioning in particular Beijing's retention of the right to revoke laws, to adjudicate cases involving defense or foreign affairs, and to interpret the Basic Law. Several local pressure groups, supported by the human rights group Amnesty International, argued that the Basic Law's guarantees on the application of two international covenants—the International Covenant on Civil and Political Rights and the International Covenant on Economic, Social and Cultural Rights, neither of which the PRC has signed—were insufficient.

The Second Draft

The PRC's response to criticisms of the Basic Law's first draft included respect for some of the opinions expressed and exasperation at residents' distrust of Chinese intentions. For example, Lu Ping, secretary-general of the Drafting Committee and deputy director of the Hong Kong and Macau Affairs Office, insisted in the face of criticism that the Basic Law's provisions on human rights were adequate.[8] However, the BLDC's subgroup considering the issue agreed to amend the provision. Several other articles that had been criticized also were amended in the second phase of the drafting process. In order to reduce the ambiguity over the relationship between national and SAR laws, drafters agreed to list in an annex the six Chinese laws that will apply to Hong Kong after 1997. Mostly symbolic, they include: (1) Resolution on the Capital, Calendar, National Anthem and National Flag, (2) Resolution on the National Day, (3) Order on the National Emblem, (4) Declaration on the Territorial Sea, (5) Nationality Law, and (6) Regulations Concerning Diplomatic Privileges and Immunities. Of these, the only potentially troublesome one concerns nationality. An article on jurisdiction was rewritten to clarify that the central government's jurisdiction will be limited to matters concerning defense and foreign affairs, while Hong Kong will maintain a court of final appeal for all other matters. The Basic Law's sweeping reference to subverting the central government was amended to require that the SAR itself enact laws prohibiting treason, secession, sedition or theft of state secrets. Finally, in response to concern over an ambiguous reference to the English language in the first draft, the second draft grants English equal status with Chinese as official languages in the SAR after 1997.

These amendments did not assuage all concerns in Hong Kong, but they nevertheless reflected a willingness on the part of mainland drafters to respond to the arguments of their Hong Kong counterparts. Li Hou, one of the top PRC drafters, explained, "The original provisions in the first draft were never intended to allow Beijing to interfere. We hope the amendments can help clear the anxieties."[9] An article published in December 1988 in the authoritative mainland journal, *Liaowang*, lauded the successes of the revision process in strengthening the SAR's guarantees of autonomy.[10]

Still, the limits to the PRC's willingness to compromise were clear. The six national laws listed in the second draft, for example, "must be applied in Hong Kong," according to the *Liaowang* article, suggesting that there was no room for further discussion. Similarly, none of the amendments to the draft Basic Law withdrew from the central government its ultimate sovereign power over Hong Kong. This is apparent in the revision of Article 169 (Article 157 in the second draft), which granted the power of interpreting the Basic Law to the NPC. The revised version retains this sentence, but a following paragraph adds the provision that the NPC may authorize Hong Kong's courts to interpret the Law. Even in this revised form, the provision does not satisfy Hong Kong liberals, who hope to preclude any possibility of interference. Mainland drafters, however, are unlikely to grant any further concessions on such a crucial issue of principle.

Political Structure

The most exacting test of Chinese intentions in the Basic Law drafting process has been the debate over political structure. The debate involves two processes: (1) the BLDC's determination of Hong Kong's post–1997 political system, which the Chinese have repeatedly insisted is a matter for China alone to settle, and (2) the Hong Kong government's reform of its existing political structure before 1997, which the Chinese have claimed is a matter for British authorities to resolve but which they have consistently attempted to influence. The two processes are intimately related, since a smooth transition in 1997 will require that the shift from colony to SAR involve as little structural change as possible.

The question of political structure has been a lightning rod for conflict within Hong Kong and between Hong Kong and Beijing. It has presented thorny problems for the Chinese, complicating their plans for a smooth transition. While formally committed to the concept of "Hong Kong people ruling Hong Kong," PRC officials have been suspicious of its more liberal formulations, demonstrating their overwhelming preference for the economic status quo and their fear of anything that might upset it. From the PRC's perspective, Hong Kong's system of colonial government, with strong central control and limited popular participation, has been part of the reason for its astounding success, and they are reluctant to see it tampered with either before or after 1997.

Chinese leaders do have some incentives to promote reform of Hong Kong's current political system, though. They must develop mechanisms to fill posts left vacant when the colonial government departs. They also recognize that the establishment of a more democratic system will reflect well on Beijing, because it will make the SAR appear more autonomous and because the Chinese will have replaced colonial rule with a democratic government.[11] Nevertheless, Chinese policy makers have clearly established the exercise of sovereignty, followed by the maintenance of stability and prosperity, as their primary goals and are extremely skeptical of any moves that would threaten them. A 1985 article in the leading PRC legal newspaper argued,

. . . Hong Kong's economy is rather fragile and cannot stand much turbulence. If there is a sudden change in the political system in Hong Kong, accompanied by a violent upheaval in its social structure, the international society will lose faith in Hong Kong and refrain from making investments and engaging in commerce and finance in Hong Kong, and the city will soon suffer from an economic depression. Therefore, the maintenance of Hong Kong's stability is of special significance in promoting the economic prosperity of Hong Kong.[12]

Chinese officials have thus shown little support for democratic reform in Hong Kong. They recognize that limited democratic mechanisms may not be bad for Hong Kong and may even be unavoidable in light of democratization that has already taken place. But Beijing's definition of democracy focuses on the inclusion in decision-making processes of a wide cross-section of society rather than on contested elections. The Chinese have taken a conservative approach to the issues of political reform and the SAR's political structure, for example by favoring an electoral college over direct elections. In this respect, they have been supported by many of Hong Kong's wealthy elite, who also fear contested elections will lead to social instability, and instability to economic decline. Thus, Xu Jiatun has expressed concern that the British government has been "pushing the representative system in Hong Kong," and warned that major political reforms would be inconsistent with the Joint Declaration. Similarly, Li Hou warned in May 1988 that Beijing reserved the right to object to any major changes in Hong Kong's political, legal, social or economic systems prior to 1997.[13]

PRC officials, in unintended concert with Hong Kong conservatives, have shown particular alarm at the prospect of political parties competing for power in Hong Kong. In June 1986, Li Hou warned that, should party politics emerge in Hong Kong, the local Chinese Communist Party branch will actively participate. One month later, Lu Ping said he thought it "better for Hong Kong that party politics do not emerge . . . One political party comes to power today and another will come to power tomorrow. This is detrimental to Hong Kong's stability."[14]

The Hong Kong government, too, has warned that "adversarial politics" may not be best for Hong Kong. However, the British are determined to leave Hong Kong with at least some democratic mechanisms in place. In fact, moves toward a more representative government in Hong Kong began well before the Sino-British agreement. Partly in response to popular pressure, the Hong Kong government in the 1970s began a gradual process of decentralizing some powers (albeit minor ones, such as management of parks, recreation and refuse) and implementing limited representative government, beginning with the Urban Council and ex-

panding to District Boards in the early 1980s. In 1985 a Regional Council
was established to provide administrative functions in the New Territories.
At the central level, the Hong Kong government increased the proportion
of unofficial members of the Legislative Council and in 1985 instituted
elections by functional constituencies for a small proportion of Legco
members. The initiation of negotiations on Hong Kong's future further
motivated the Hong Kong government to implement democratic reforms,
in the hope that a limited democratic system would help keep Beijing
from manipulating Hong Kong's internal affairs after 1997.[15]

But the British desire to take the lead in instituting political reforms
before 1997 has been tempered by their preference for gradual changes
and their desire to placate Chinese concerns on this issue in order to
insure a smooth transition. In a step that was widely seen as a victory
for the Chinese, the JLG in November 1985 adopted political reform as
a topic for discussion. Later, it became apparent that the Hong Kong
government was prepared to consult Chinese officials before undertaking
further political reforms.[16]

The British side also took the initiative in proposing a plan for the
transition from colonial to SAR government. Governor Wilson first
proposed a "through-train" model, by which a government put in place
in 1995 would continue to serve until 1999, thereby minimizing the
logistical difficulties of the transition. The Chinese rejected this approach
on the grounds that it placed in British hands the right to establish the
first SAR government. They were more receptive to a second proposal,
dubbed the "Lo Wu solution," a reference to the border town where
passengers on local trains to and from the mainland disembark, clear
customs, then walk across the border. According to this proposal, the
Hong Kong Legislative Council, selected in 1995, would be dissolved
on July 1, 1997. Members would immediately take an oath of allegiance
to the PRC, after which they would be sworn in as members of the
first Hong Kong SAR Legislative Council. In order to make the transition
even smoother, the SAR's first chief executive would be named sometime
in 1996. In this way, continuity could be maintained through the transfer,
but the formalities of establishing the first SAR government would remain
in Chinese hands. Beijing agreed in principle to the Lo Wu solution in
November 1988.[17]

The question of exactly how the SAR government will be selected is
far more complex and is an extremely sensitive issue for both Hong
Kong and the PRC. The Basic Law's first draft reached no conclusion
on the issue, offering instead five alternatives for selecting the chief
executive and members of the Legislative Council. The major differences
among the proposals concerned the extension of suffrage and the relative
roles of electoral college, functional constituencies and general election

in the selection of officeholders. The issue has sparked heated public debate and protest in Hong Kong, where conservative groups have favored limited suffrage and a gradual transition to general election, while liberals have championed a faster transition to election on a one person, one vote basis. Attempts at mediation between the two sides have achieved little success. In November 1988, the well-known publisher of Hong Kong's *Ming Pao* and a co-convener of the BLDC's subgroup on political structure, Louis Cha, attempted to resolve the indecision by submitting a proposal for gradual transition. Known as the "mainstream proposal," it calls for the number of directly elected Legco members to be increased to fifty percent over three terms, or twelve years. The SAR's chief executive would be elected by an 800-member electoral college for the first three five-year terms, after which a territory-wide referendum would be held to determine whether general elections should be instituted. Liberal leaders argued that this proposal moved too slowly toward democracy. After the BLDC's subgroup on the political system passed the proposal in early December, liberal groups protested publicly, staging a twenty-four hour hunger strike and a ceremonial burning of the draft Basic Law.

The Chinese response to the debate over alternatives for representative government has included limited tolerance for discussion of elections coupled with fear that democratic reforms may go "too far." During the Sino-British negotiations, several Chinese officials indicated that the Hong Kong SAR's top officials would be chosen through elections, and that notion eventually was enshrined in the Joint Declaration. In discussions surrounding the Basic Law, PRC officials commonly have accepted the likelihood that Hong Kong's post–1997 political structure will involve elections of some type. In February 1989, Xu Jiatun said in a speech before the NPC Standing Committee that Hong Kong must develop a democratic system with broad participation. "A local consensus is that the territory must develop democracy. A democratic political system is a must in order to implement a high degree of autonomy and the policy of 'Hong Kong people ruling Hong Kong.'"[18] And although Chinese officials have expressed skepticism regarding the formation of political parties in Hong Kong, they have not ruled it out entirely. Xu Jiatun said in January and February 1989 that Hong Kong people were free to organize political parties, on one occasion explaining that this right was guaranteed through the right of association in the Basic Law.[19]

At times, however, top PRC officials have retreated from that position. In November 1985, Xu Jiatun caused alarm in Hong Kong when he criticized British attempts to develop representative government in the colony, accusing them of "current tendencies to deviate" from the Joint Declaration and warning that "unfortunate consequences" would result.[20]

In May 1987, Deng Xiaoping reversed earlier official positions when he said, in reference to plans for elections, "I'm afraid it won't suit Hong Kong to copy all this Western stuff."[21]

Chinese policy makers appear willing to accept limited democracy in Hong Kong. They also recognize that any attempt to destroy democratic reforms before 1997 would cause a public uproar and disrupt the transition process that they are so anxious to see proceed smoothly. Chinese officials' tolerance on this issue is limited by two factors, however. First, they are unwilling to let the British impose unilaterally a political structure that would be carried over to the SAR. If there is to be democracy in Hong Kong, it is to be a product of Chinese initiative rather than Great Britain's parting gift to the colony. Thus, Chinese criticism of political reform proposals has been strongest when they have interpreted them as threats to their resumption of sovereignty. Hong Kong's political reform and the SAR's proposed political structure, they have argued, should "converge." Indeed, the PRC has warned that any reforms which go beyond the Basic Law's provisions will be unilaterally altered after 1997.

Second, the Chinese are concerned that "too much" democracy "too fast" will upset the economic climate by inviting political confrontation and opportunism. Thus, while they have occasionally made conciliatory gestures to liberal demands, Chinese officials have consistently favored conservative proposals. In his speech before the NPC calling for a democratic system in Hong Kong, for example, Xu Jiatun qualified his statements in an important way: "Given democracy is new to the territory, there has to be a procedure through which to develop democracy. Drastic reforms are impossible, only gradual and prudent changes."[22] Mainland members of the BLDC therefore were quick to endorse adoption of the conservative "mainstream proposal" in the Basic Law's second draft. In an interesting twist of logic, mainland drafter Li Hou pointed out that the existence of both conservative and liberal opposition to the proposal simply proved that it was the best alternative.[23] Crucial to the success of any proposal, however, will be whether liberal activists continue to agitate for broader democratic reforms, putting additional pressure on the Chinese and British in the run-up to 1997.

The Transition: A Test of Chinese Policy

The process of drafting the Basic Law and settling the long list of political and economic arrangements related to the transition of sovereignty has forced Chinese policy makers for the first time to reconcile principle with practice in Hong Kong. This has not been easy. The PRC's preliminary steps to establish "one country, two systems," and "Hong

Kong people ruling Hong Kong" have met with unexpected difficulties caused by the unique nature of the Hong Kong question and the unprecedented nature of its proposed solution.

The PRC has insisted on its intention to adhere to the spirit of the Joint Declaration. But whereas officials in London and Hong Kong see the essence of the Joint Declaration to be its promise of SAR autonomy and the continued status quo, the Chinese consider the recovery of sovereignty to be its primary element. Thus, any suggestion that the transition from colony to SAR be designed in a way that leaves the British a prominent role has been flatly rejected. Likewise, the Chinese have refused to consider any suggestion that the Hong Kong SAR be removed from the ultimate control of Beijing. From the PRC's perspective, Hong Kong is not a separate country that has chosen to unite with the PRC, and its promised autonomy should not be construed as granting Hong Kong equal status with the central government.

Within the context established by these non-negotiable items, the Chinese have shown considerable flexibility. The Basic Law, in spite of its shortcomings, grants a substantial degree of autonomy to the SAR. Furthermore, Chinese drafters responded to several key concerns expressed during the first period of consultation, incorporating major changes in the second draft that increased the SAR's formal autonomy. These include crucial articles concerning jurisdiction, legislative powers and human rights. Even on the difficult issue of nationality, several Chinese officials suggested that some means could be worked out to circumvent Chinese nationality law and allow Hong Kong residents with foreign passports to hold public office in the SAR.

The period of transition in the 1990s will provide a continuing test of the Chinese commitment to their stated goals. The PRC has promised that its policy toward Hong Kong during the transition will be guided by two principles: transfer of sovereignty and stable transition of government. While the first principle is no doubt primary in Chinese minds, there is sufficient reason to trust their intention to abide by the second as well. This will be difficult, however. Political developments in Hong Kong, including popular activism, may lead officials in Beijing to see either China's sovereignty or Hong Kong's economic stability threatened, and they may be tempted to interfere in the colony's affairs by applying pressure on the Hong Kong government through official and unofficial channels. Any such actions by the PRC would likely cause alarm among Hong Kong residents, creating an atmosphere of even greater uncertainty and tension. Political reform is the most pressing issue over which such problems may arise, and the PRC has already demonstrated its preference for economic stability over democracy in Hong Kong. This issue will continue to provide the most revealing indications not only of Chinese leaders' intentions to abide by the Joint Declaration, but of their capacity to accept the potentially unpleasant results of doing so.

Democracy and the June Fourth Incident

In such a politically sensitive atmosphere, it is not surprising that China's student-led movement for political reform in the spring of 1989 electrified Hong Kong. Residents organized in support of the students' cause, making Hong Kong the top supplier of financial support to the demonstrators in Beijing. Several rallies were held in support of the students occupying Tiananmen Square and participation reached unprecedented levels for Hong Kong, at times as many as one million people.

The brutal massacre and ensuing crackdown in June 1989 that crushed the movement in the PRC shocked Hong Kong's residents. Many continued their activism by organizing information campaigns that attempted to circumvent the central government's propaganda whitewash by sending photocopies of Hong Kong newspaper accounts to mainland residents. Politicians in Hong Kong and London called for Great Britain to rethink its commitment to the Joint Declaration, and several members of the Basic Law Drafting and Consultative Committees resigned or suspended their work. Pro-China Hong Kong newspapers broke ranks with the PRC's propaganda line, and several prominent conservatives who had opposed a rapid transition to democracy changed their stances in favor of more liberal proposals. There also was an increase in popular demands that Great Britain grant right of abode to Hong Kong holders of BNO passports. The British government appeared unwilling to concede on that issue, but it moved to support more rapid democratization in Hong Kong, proposed the introduction of a Bill of Rights in the colony, and publicly questioned whether PLA troops should be stationed in the SAR. This set off a new round of accusations between China and Britain that damaged the atmosphere of bilateral consultation and cooperation.

Though PRC officials moved quickly to reassure Hong Kong residents that China's policy toward Hong Kong remained unchanged, the tragic events in Beijing had created daunting new problems for Chinese relations with the colony. Hong Kong residents, many of whom already doubted whether the Chinese leadership would permit democracy in Hong Kong, saw little hope for Hong Kong's political reforms after the violent suppression of peaceful demonstrations on the mainland. The Basic Law drafting process, which had been proceeding relatively smoothly, was damaged severely, as Hong Kong drafters prepared to demand stronger guarantees of local autonomy. And no matter what the final outcome of the drafting process, the colony's residents had gained new reasons to doubt the PRC's commitment to carrying out its promises. Applications to emigrate grew dramatically, intensifying Hong Kong's "brain drain" problem.

Similarly, whatever legitimacy China's post-Mao leadership had gained among Hong Kong residents since the institution of economic reforms was quickly destroyed, and the PRC's extensive United Front campaign to gain support for its Hong Kong policy lost its persuasive power. These developments weakened the Chinese leadership's appeals to Hong Kong residents on patriotic grounds and made the task of winning support for future Chinese policy proposals enormously difficult. Where once people had hoped for Deng Xiaoping's continued presence at the top of the Chinese leadership in order to help assure Hong Kong's prosperity, they now called for his ouster and the downfall of the central government.

Incentives for Chinese Policy Makers

The likelihood that Beijing will take measures that will upset Hong Kong's stability in the years before 1997 is difficult to predict. One can at least identify continuing incentives for Chinese officials to acquiesce to the political preferences of Hong Kong elites and to abstain from obvious interference in Hong Kong's internal disputes. The most prominent of those incentives is economic. While Basic Law drafters argued over Hong Kong's future political, economic and social systems, the PRC's economic interests in the colony continued to grow at a rapid pace. Spurred by relaxed investment regulations, mainland firms at the central, provincial and municipal levels invested heavily in the colony. In 1985, the PRC became Hong Kong's largest trading partner, and in 1986 China replaced Great Britain as the third largest foreign investor in Hong Kong manufacturing, after the United States and Japan. In 1988, total Chinese investment in Hong Kong was estimated at US$6 billion, and four thousand mainland Chinese were stationed in the colony. While precise figures are unavailable, it was estimated that the PRC had interests in at least 3000 Hong Kong firms.[24] The Bank of China Group continued to elevate its own profile in the colony by investing heavily in Hong Kong manufacturing, increasing its loans to Hong Kong firms for investment in the PRC, and constructing a seventy-story, US$260 million headquarters designed by the famed architect, I. M. Pei. By mid-1986, the Bank of China had become Hong Kong's second largest bank, behind the Hong Kong and Shanghai Banking Corporation.

Joint-venture investment with Hong Kong firms, mainly in coastal provinces, also continued to grow. Hong Kong provided two-thirds of all joint-venture investment capital in China and fully ninety percent in the Shenzhen Special Economic Zone.[25] An estimated three million workers in the Canton Delta region were engaged in producing goods for Hong Kong firms. The most highly publicized joint venture was a US$3.5 billion deal with Hong Kong's China Light and Power Company to build a nuclear power plant thirty miles northeast of Hong Kong at Daya Bay in Guangdong. The contract was signed in January 1985, but the project encountered strong public opposition after the Chernobyl disaster in April 1986 awakened the Hong Kong public to the dangers of nuclear power plants. Eventually the Chinese agreed to establish a consultative committee of Hong Kong and mainland residents to discuss safety concerns at the plant, and the public outcry diminished. Work on the project began in August 1987, and the plant was scheduled to begin generating electricity, more than half of which would go to Hong Kong, in 1992.

China's growing involvement in Hong Kong's economy had a negative side as well. Mainlanders with little experience in capitalist systems made costly bad investments, and many of their firms in Hong Kong went into debt. Even Wang Guangying, whose entrance into the Hong Kong business world as head of Everbright Corporation brought such attention, later turned out to be less sophisticated than many people in the colony had originally thought.[26] It also became apparent by 1988 that some mainland Chinese were engaging in corrupt practices in Hong Kong, including embezzlement and money laundering. In an attempt to deal with this problem, Hong Kong's NCNA branch established an internal watchdog agency to monitor the actions of mainland firms in the colony.

Hong Kong's long-standing role as a door to Western technology and ideas continued to grow through the late 1980s. Even as the mainland became more accessible to foreigners, Hong Kong was still recognized as a superior location for business and other contacts, and the rising number of mainland visitors to the colony, already close to 300,000 per year in 1986, reflected this. Many of the visitors were on tours that offered a first-hand look at capitalist economics or advanced management techniques. In August 1988, the PRC opened the Beijing–Hong Kong Economic Research Centre Ltd., established to train Chinese officials from coastal regions in the rudiments of capitalism. The Centre's general manager explained that Hong Kong was "the most appropriate place to conduct the training because it has been very successful in developing capitalism."[27] The PRC in January 1989 also announced plans for officials to visit Hong Kong to study how the colony trains its civil servants, so that similar methods could be employed in the PRC.[28]

External relations also continued to influence Chinese calculations. Official organs publicized Chinese concessions during the Basic Law drafting process, arguing that they reflected China's sensitivity to Hong

Kong's unusual circumstances (and perhaps revealing that they were less concessionary than mainland drafters would have others believe). While such propaganda was in part directed at reassuring Hong Kong residents, it was also intended for the foreign audience and for Taiwan. The question of Taiwan's reunification with the mainland differs in significant ways from that of Hong Kong's, but Chinese officials continue to maintain that Taiwan also can become an SAR of China.[29] They recognize further that a successful transition in Hong Kong will be a public relations bonanza for the reunification cause.

Key elements of the historical Chinese calculus on Hong Kong have thus remained in place following the signing of the Sino-British agreement. But that calculus has also grown more complex as the PRC has been forced to deal with the details of the Basic Law, the transfer of sovereignty and political reform. PRC officials claim that their positions on these matters have been and will continue to be guided by the principles set forth in the Joint Declaration. Yet those principles may not always be mutually consistent. During the transition period, and certainly after 1997, Chinese leaders will be pressured to choose between their promises of stability and democracy, or between Chinese sovereignty and local autonomy. The Basic Law drafting process has revealed that all principles are not necessarily equal. Within the non-negotiable context of Chinese sovereignty, mainland drafters have been most accommodating on issues related to Hong Kong's economic prosperity, but they have been less tolerant of proposals for political liberalization or human rights guarantees. There are important incentives for the PRC to maintain Hong Kong's status quo, and Chinese leaders have demonstrated that they are committed to doing so. As 1997 approaches, however, they may be forced to demonstrate whether they are more committed to some aspects of that status quo than others.

Notes

1. See Norman Miners, "The Normal Pattern of Decolonization of British Dependent Territories," in Peter Wesley-Smith and Albert Chen, eds., *The Basic Law and Hong Kong's Future* (Hong Kong: Butterworths, 1988): 44–54.

2. On the creation and early meetings of the BLDC, see Emily Lau, "The Early History of the Drafting Process," in Wesley-Smith and Chen, eds., *The Basic Law*, 90–104.

3. The description of these events draws heavily on Lau, "Early History."

4. *Hong Kong Standard (Standard)*, Aug. 27, 1986, in Foreign Broadcast Information Service (FBIS), *Daily Report: China*, Aug. 28, 1986, W4–7.

5. *People's Daily*, Sept. 28 and 29, 1984.

6. *New China News Agency (NCNA)*, July 18, 1986, in FBIS, July 24, 1986, E3–5.

7. *South China Morning Post (Post),* Nov. 18, 1988, in FBIS, Nov. 18, 1988, 60.

8. *Post,* Nov. 24, 1988, in FBIS, Nov. 28, 1988, 69–70.

9. *Post,* Nov. 18, 1988, in FBIS, Nov. 18, 1988, 59.

10. See *Liaowang,* no. 49 (Dec. 5, 1988): 21–22.

11. For a discussion of British and Chinese attitudes toward political reform in Hong Kong, see Lau Siu-kai, "Political Reform and Political Development in Hong Kong: Dilemmas and Choices," in Y.C. Jao, et. al, eds., *Hong Kong and 1997: Strategies for the Future* (Hong Kong: Centre of Asian Studies, University of Hong Kong, 1985): 23–49.

12. *Zhongguo Fazhi Bao* [China Legal News], Jan. 25, 1985, in FBIS, Feb. 4, 1985, E3.

13. *Ta Kung Pao,* Nov. 28 to Dec. 4, 1985, in FBIS, Dec. 3, 1985, W1–4; *Post,* May 19, 1988, in FBIS, May 25, 1988, 56–57.

14. *Post,* June 3, 1986, in FBIS, June 4, 1986, W5–7; *Hsin Wan Pao,* July 2, 1986, in FBIS, July 9, 1986, W5.

15. See Lau Siu-kai and Kuan Hsin-chi, "Hong Kong After the Sino-British Agreement: Limits to Change," *Pacific Affairs* 59, no. 2 (Summer 1986): 214–236.

16. Lau and Kuan, "Hong Kong," 222.

17. *Post,* Nov. 4, 1988, in FBIS, Nov. 4, 1981, 56–57; *Post,* Nov. 19, 1988, in FBIS, Nov. 23, 1988, 66–67.

18. *Post,* Feb. 21, 1989, in FBIS, Feb. 22, 1989, 56–57.

19. *Standard,* Jan. 27, 1989, in FBIS, Jan. 27, 1989, 74; *Standard,* Jan. 5, 1989, in FBIS, Jan. 5, 1989, 71.

20. *Asian Wall Street Journal (AWSJ),* Nov. 25, 1985.

21. *AWSJ,* May 26, 1987.

22. *Post,* Feb. 21, 1989, in FBIS, Feb. 22, 1989, 65–67.

23. *Liaowang,* no. 49 (Dec. 5, 1988): 21–22, in FBIS, Dec. 14, 1988, 5.

24. *AWSJ,* Feb. 9. 1987; *Standard,* May 20, 1988, in FBIS, May 26, 1988, 55; *Standard,* May 26, 1988, in FBIS, May 26, 1988, 56–57.

25. Graham E. Johnson, "1997 and After: Will Hong Kong Survive? A Personal View," *Pacific Affairs* 59, no. 2 (Summer 1986): 245; *Kuang Chiao Ching* [Wide Angle] 165 (June 16, 1982): 28–31, in FBIS, June 30, 1986, W1–8.

26. *AWSJ,* April 28, 1986.

27. *Standard,* Oct. 12, 1988, in FBIS, Oct. 13, 1988, 87–88.

28. *Standard,* Jan 4, 1989, in FBIS, Jan 5, 1989, 73.

29. Taiwan's status is not affected by the existence of a treaty, nor is the island administered by foreign authorities who would "return" it to the PRC. Taiwan, which enjoys strong defense forces and a healthy economy, is ruled by a KMT-led government that still claims the right to authority over all of China. Any proposal for peaceful reunification would require approval by the KMT, which consistently has rejected the possibility of accepting the CCP's authority, even with promises of administrative autonomy on Taiwan.

7

1997 and Beyond

Lessons of History

In the lively debate over Hong Kong's future, there has been a tendency to label its participants as either optimists or pessimists.[1] In the popular view, optimists expect that Hong Kong's lifestyle and economy will not be substantially altered after its return to Chinese sovereignty. They focus on the PRC's incentives, particularly economic ones, for maintaining Hong Kong's status quo, arguing that Chinese leaders will do everything in their power to avoid even the appearance of meddling in Hong Kong after 1997 for fear of sparking a crisis of confidence that would destroy the territory's economy.

Pessimists, on the other hand, put little faith in Chinese promises. Pointing to Shanghai's economic collapse after the Communist takeover, they argue that Hong Kong is likely to suffer a similar fate. Chinese officials have duped and pressured the British into an agreement that gives the PRC full authority in Hong Kong after 1997, they say. PRC officials will be unable to avoid intervening in the territory's affairs after 1997, and as a result of either evil intent or simple incompetence, they will frighten away investment, restrict civil rights and generally remake Hong Kong in the image of the mainland.

Most opinions on Hong Kong's future fall somewhere between the two extremes. Many observers believe that the current PRC leadership does not intend to harm Hong Kong, but they caution that Chinese officials might make mistakes in implementing their "one country, two systems" policy, or point out that Hong Kong will suffer if the priorities of economic reform on the mainland are altered substantially. They welcome provisions for Hong Kong's autonomy but fear that when central government and SAR policies come into conflict, the SAR's autonomy may turn out to be hollow.

An understanding of the history of Chinese policy toward Hong Kong cannot provide the answers that will end speculation on the colony's future. It can, however, help clarify the issues involved. In trying to understand future PRC policy toward Hong Kong, the distinction between optimists and pessimists is analytically meaningless. The crucial task, rather, is to recognize policy alternatives and to assess the factors that will motivate PRC policy makers in choosing among them.

Realizing Sovereignty

At the center of any future Hong Kong policy will be the expression of sovereignty, which must include the absolute authority of the central government and the absence of any third party involvement in the territory's administration. In the past, Chinese officials have reacted strongly to any perceived challenges, even symbolic ones, to their sovereignty in Hong Kong, and they are likely to continue to do so in the future. Even after Hong Kong's "unequal treaties" have been annulled, the sting of their legacy still will be felt.

The pursuit of sovereignty over Hong Kong has meant different things at different times. To the Nationalists, it was an achievable goal, an integral if not central element of the larger project to regain Chinese territorial integrity through the renegotiation of unequal treaties. The Communists after 1949 had more modest aims, choosing to maintain their claims to sovereignty but refraining from acting on those claims, at least in the short term. On those occasions when it was forced to take a stand, the PRC merely deferred resolution of the matter to a point in the distant future, when conditions would be ripe.

However, once sovereignty was placed on the bargaining table, beginning formally with Prime Minister Thatcher's 1982 visit to Beijing, the PRC's claim to sovereignty took on a new urgency. Thatcher aggravated the situation by taking a hard-line stance on the treaties and on the importance of British administration in the territory, which appeared to Chinese leaders as an attempt to continue imperialism in Hong Kong. Had the British approach been more conciliatory from the start, for example by renouncing British sovereignty and admitting to the imposition of treaty terms on the Qing government, Chinese leaders would likely have been more receptive to other British concerns and less suspicious of British intentions during the negotiations and the transition period.[2] Nevertheless, PRC leaders still would have found it necessary to stand firm on sovereignty once it became apparent that the issue could no longer be sidestepped.

During the remaining years of transition, sovereignty will continue to be a sensitive issue. Hong Kong's liberal activists, and to a lesser extent the British government, will want to test the limits of the SAR's autonomy guarantee, while PRC leaders will continue to remind them that Hong Kong is not being granted independence. The Chinese leadership has already shown impatience with some demands, for example by refusing to accept compulsory jurisdiction of the International Court of Justice in disputes concerning implementation of the Joint Declaration. Beijing will be particularly suspicious of accelerated moves toward democratization, which it may view as a plot to limit the PRC's authority after 1997.

After Hong Kong becomes an SAR, the issue of sovereignty will acquire still another dimension. Technically, the problem should no longer exist once British administration is ended. Nevertheless, Great Britain will monitor carefully the implementation of the Joint Declaration and may choose to dispute certain aspects of it. That would create a difficult problem for Chinese officials, who have claimed both that the Joint Declaration is a legally binding international agreement and that Hong Kong's status is a matter for the PRC government alone to settle. More important, with the British gone the Chinese central government will be forced to establish the working parameters of Hong Kong's autonomy. The Joint Declaration and the Basic Law provide mechanisms for the central government to exert its control, including the NPC's formal appointment of top SAR officials, its right to amend laws, and its right to interpret the Basic Law. Should the leadership in Beijing object to any developments in the SAR, it may be tempted to use those mechanisms to assert its control directly.

Chinese leaders have historically been willing to accommodate the unusual circumstances of Hong Kong's status. But that accommodation has not been absolute. Chinese officials have on occasion expressed disagreement with Hong Kong government policies or have supported disruptive movements in the colony. They have also insisted that activity in Hong Kong not pose a threat to the mainland. In this respect, the Hong Kong government has been willing to oblige, by controlling political activity that could be perceived as threatening to China, and in most cases, making sure that Hong Kong was a "good neighbor." The Hong Kong government banished Sun Yat-sen from the colony in 1891, for example, explaining that "this government has no intention of allowing the British colony of Hong Kong to be used as an asylum for persons engaged in plots and dangerous conspiracies against a friendly neighboring Empire. . . ."[3] During the ten years that the Nationalists were firmly in power, Communist activity in the colony was squelched, and after the establishment of the PRC, anti-Communist propaganda was controlled. In addition, Great Britain in February 1950 was among the first countries to recognize the new Communist government. Under these circumstances, as long as the "status quo" has posed no real threat to China, Chinese leaders have been willing to compromise their principles, at least in the short term, and to allow Hong Kong to prosper under British rule.

An International Question

Chinese accommodation of Hong Kong reflects policy makers' assessment of several key aspects of the colony's status. One of these is the international nature of the Hong Kong issue. The KMT was particularly concerned about the effects its actions toward Hong Kong might have on Sino-British relations and on China's international reputation. Even with American backing, Chiang Kai-shek was unable to convince the British to return Hong Kong, and he was not inclined to risk the diplomatic opprobrium that would follow any attempt to stir unrest in the colony or recover it militarily. Communist officials after 1949 have shown less explicit concern than the Nationalists for good relations with the U.S. and Great Britain, but they have demonstrated a similar concern over international reaction to Chinese foreign policy initiatives. And despite their claim that Hong Kong is Chinese territory that can be recovered at any time, they have clearly recognized that causing disruption in the colony would bring international embarrassment.

After 1997, Hong Kong will remain an international center for trade and finance with a large foreign population and substantial foreign investment. Policy toward Hong Kong therefore will in some sense continue to be an "international" issue for the PRC. Chinese officials have shown that they value the territory's sizable foreign investment, whose importance increased with the outflow of local capital that began in the 1980s, by repeatedly reassuring foreign investors that their interests will be protected. The Joint Declaration includes provisions for the retention of foreign nationals in public service and states that Hong Kong will remain an international financial center. The Basic Law also includes provisions designed to maintain foreign interests in the territory.

However, the absence after 1997 of the "buffer" provided by British rule will represent a major qualitative adjustment to Hong Kong's international status. The PRC's leaders will be in a position to adopt policies that will impact directly on foreigners and foreign investment in Hong Kong. In addition, the importance of foreign investment to Hong Kong's economy after 1997 will not necessarily prevent Beijing from interfering in the SAR's internal affairs. Increased limitations on the civil rights of Hong Kong residents, for example, would likely have little effect on foreign investors, whose main purpose in Hong Kong is, and will be, to make money. Policies that damaged the SAR's economy would certainly cause concern in the foreign community, but most foreign investors could depart Hong Kong quickly, moving a large portion of their assets electronically. Hong Kong is to remain an international community, but no one will dispute Chinese sovereignty there, nor will an international outcry be particulary effective if the central government causes, wittingly or not, the territory's economic demise. In addition, the crackdown on China's democracy movement in 1989 proved that PRC leaders are not always sensitive to international reaction, particularly when they can claim that an issue is an "internal affair."

Chinese leaders are especially concerned with the reaction their Hong Kong policy brings in Taiwan. Despite ample skepticism in Taipei, PRC officials have consistently claimed that "one country, two systems" is a workable model for national reunification because it allows capitalist and socialist systems to exist side by side. They recognize that reunification with Taiwan will be more complex but insist that the main elements of the Hong Kong solution are applicable. In a 1985 speech before the NPC, Xu Jiatun asked, "Concerning the issue of Taiwan's return to the motherland, what even particularly complex problems cannot be solved through negotiations as long as Taiwan's capitalism is unchanged by the mainland's socialism and vice versa?"[4] Such a statement simplifies drastically the PRC-Taiwan reunification problem and can hardly be taken seriously in Taipei, but it does indicate that the Chinese leadership is anxious to demonstrate that its Hong Kong solution can work. That concern may provide the PRC with a continuing incentive for moderation.

A Door to the World

PRC officials also hope to maintain Hong Kong's stability and prosperity in order to continue to utilize the territory's long-standing role as a point of access to the West. Just as Hong Kong's cession provided the British a toehold in China, so the colony quickly became recognized in the mainland as a place for contact with the outside world. This had an impact not only on trade, but also on the development of modern Chinese culture and society.

Since the late 1970s, officials in Beijing have acknowledged the significance they attach to Hong Kong's role as a "door to the world." The colony provides a convenient location for the acquisition of technology, expertise, and trade contacts that are essential to the Four Modernizations program. Its location also facilitates trade and contact with foreign countries with which the PRC does not have diplomatic relations, as well as with Taiwan, which has in recent years seen its trade with the mainland, most of which is conducted through Hong Kong, expand dramatically. The PRC has sent numerous trade delegations to Hong Kong and has held an increasing number of trade shows in the colony in recent years. No city on the mainland can compete with modern, efficient Hong Kong in facilitating trade contacts, and PRC officials have expressed their willingness to maintain this characteristic of the territory after the British depart. There will be some complications in this respect, as countries that do not have diplomatic relations with the PRC will be required to revise the status of their missions in Hong Kong, but such changes should not present serious problems and PRC officials have indicated that they will be cooperative.

The further opening of China's major coastal cities eventually might draw foreigners away from Hong Kong, but this is not likely in the near term. Since the PRC began its economic liberalization in the late 1970s, Hong Kong's importance in facilitating contacts has grown. Chinese officials realize that it will take several decades, even at rapid growth rates, for the PRC to offer the kind of environment for foreigners that Hong Kong now provides.

Hong Kong's cosmopolitan environment will also create new problems for the PRC, however. Since its inception, Hong Kong has provided access not only to those looking to enter China, but also to those trying to escape. It has been the major point of exit for political and economic refugees, most from neighboring Guangdong. After 1997, Hong Kong will continue to be a preferred destination for Chinese on the mainland who hope for a higher standard of living, but the PRC plans to maintain existing borders and will need to strictly control access to the SAR.

The PRC is also likely to exert some control over political activity in the SAR. The civil rights guarantees included in the Joint Declaration and the Basic Law will not extend to people who publicly oppose or threaten the PRC. The British administration in the colony has always kept a close eye on activities that could anger the government across the border, but internal control will almost certainly become tighter after 1997, since the central government has little to gain from allowing opposition political activities in the territory.

The Economic Imperative

PRC officials expect Hong Kong to continue to generate substantial economic benefits after 1997, just as it has in the past. For the KMT, Hong Kong was a major entrepôt port and a source of funds. For the Communists, Hong Kong has also served a useful entrepôt role, though in recent years the PRC's financial interests in the colony have broadened considerably. In the course of negotiating the Sino-British agreement and drafting the Basic Law, Chinese officials have demonstrated great concern for the territory's future economic health. They have been reluctant to change those aspects of Hong Kong's current society, such as its common law legal system, which they see as fundamental to the territory's stable conduct of business. An article in the PRC's *China Legal News* argued that, "Only when the various existing basic systems implemented in Hong Kong are retained will it be possible to maintain and develop its prosperity. It is precisely based on such needs that the Chinese government has proposed the wise strategic decision of one country, two systems."[5]

Hong Kong's economic relationship with the mainland will not necessarily be sufficient to guarantee the continuation of its existing social, legal and economic systems, however. The PRC has made it absolutely clear that economic considerations will be subordinate to the preservation of Chinese sovereignty after 1997 and, if the central government feels threatened by developments in the territory, it could take measures that would harm the economy. It is also possible that, in their zealousness to protect Hong Kong's "stability and prosperity," Chinese leaders will unwittingly do just the opposite. During the economic crisis that accompanied the first stage of the Sino-British negotiations, for example, Beijing called repeatedly for intervention by the Hong Kong government to stop the fall of the Hong Kong dollar. The government itself later intervened, but leaders in Beijing were far more willing to take quick and dramatic measures. After 1997, the Chinese central government might feel compelled to intervene quickly to halt an economic downturn in Hong Kong, with the unintended result of undermining confidence among foreign and local investors. Such a situation would be exacerbated by the pervasive skepticism in Hong Kong regarding Beijing's motives. Investors and residents would probably move quickly to exercise any available option to depart the territory, creating a crisis atmosphere.

Competing Concerns

Despite the incentives that will push the PRC toward moderation in its post–1997 Hong Kong policy, there already have been indications that concern for maintaining the status quo does not extend consistently to all areas of Hong Kong society. PRC officials have been most accommodative in those areas that appear to hold direct relevance to the territory's economy. The continuation of Hong Kong's status as a free port and an international financial center with a capitalist economic system were among the earliest promises to be leaked from Beijing before Thatcher's 1982 visit. After the agreement was signed, the JLG was able to reach agreement quickly on Hong Kong's participation in a long list of international organizations, including the General Agreement on Tariffs and Trade, the Multifiber Arrangement and the Customs Cooperation Council. In the Basic Law drafting process, too, mainland drafters have been far more understanding of Hong Kong's concerns over economic provisions than political ones. And their concessions on matters of political reform appear to have come after they were persuaded that insufficient reform could have negative economic effects. After the PRC in January 1987 moderated its opposition to direct elections, one official Chinese source was reported to have said, "We are not against democracy, but we are concerned that radical reforms should not lead to confrontational politics in Hong Kong because the success of the territory hinges on stability and prosperity."[6]

After 1997, demands for political reform and civil rights guarantees may come into conflict with what Beijing perceives as its territorial rights and the SAR's economic interests. The record thus far suggests that in the absence of such conflict, central government officials will see no need to interfere in the territory's affairs and will honor the guarantees provided in the Basic Law. Should a serious conflict emerge, however, the PRC's Hong Kong policy will likely aim first to eliminate any threat to sovereignty, then to prevent damage to the territory's economy. Other concerns rank farther down the list of priorities.

The issue of competing imperatives in China's Hong Kong policy has not been addressed publicly by Chinese officials, yet it poses a potentially serious threat to the successful implementation of the Joint Declaration. Chinese officials may indeed be sincere in supporting the goals for Hong Kong's future outlined in the Joint Declaration and the Basic Law, but those goals are not necessarily consistent. As in any society, tradeoffs will be made, generating conflict and requiring further compromise.

Looking to the Future

Domestic Politics and Hong Kong

PRC policy toward Hong Kong in the future will to some extent reflect the nation's internal political developments. Should the current economic reform program continue in the same broad direction it followed in the 1980s, toward greater liberalization of domestic economic regulations and increased reliance on foreign investment, Hong Kong's value to the mainland will continue to grow. Even if the reforms are moderated, as they were in the late 1980s, the Chinese leadership will likely continue to grant Hong Kong a central role in the nation's modernization drive. Should the reform program be reversed or substantially altered in a conservative direction, however, Beijing's perception of Hong Kong's value may change, altering the calculus for Chinese policy makers and diminishing the importance of maintaining the SAR's economic strength.

But the extent to which Hong Kong's future is to be held hostage to shifting political winds in Beijing has been overstated. Over the past several decades, Chinese policy toward Hong Kong has remained fundamentally consistent in the face of all but the most radical swings in policy. Once Hong Kong's affairs become a "domestic" issue, of course, the territory will become far more vulnerable. It will be an obvious target for anticapitalist and antiforeign movements of the type that have been undertaken on several occasions since 1949, and it may become the subject of policy battles in Beijing in ways that it never could have while under British control. Some Chinese officials have objected to the import of "corrupting" influences from the colony, for example, and they may feel emboldened to voice their objections more loudly after 1997.

Still, short of a return to Cultural Revolution radicalism, Chinese leaders in the future can be expected to recognize the advantages of honoring the Joint Declaration and preserving Hong Kong's autonomy, even if the SAR's economic benefits to the mainland decline in importance. Though technically a domestic issue, Hong Kong's internal affairs will remain fundamentally different in status from those of other Chinese provinces, municipalities and Special Economic Zones, creating a political barrier to central government intervention that, while not impregnable, nevertheless should not be penetrated as a matter of course. Thus, policy shifts in Beijing will be of concern in Hong Kong but will not necessarily cause major disruptions. And just as the continued influence of Deng Xiaoping does not guarantee Hong Kong's future, nor is there reason to expect that a transfer of authority will sound Hong Kong's death knell.

The Transition Period

The Chinese and British governments have agreed on the "transfer of sovereignty" and a "smooth transition" as guiding principles for the period leading up to 1997. PRC officials have shown that they take both principles seriously. They have reacted strongly to perceived slights of Chinese sovereignty by the British or by Hong Kong interest groups and frequently have expressed concern for the territory's economic stability. The area of greatest attention has been, and will continue to be, political reform in Hong Kong. Officials in Beijing have indicated that they do not trust the British to maintain the territory's stability or to respect the PRC's interests in Hong Kong's political developments. They suspect the British of undertaking a last-ditch effort to establish democratic institutions, leaving Beijing to pick up the pieces after 1997. They see such moves as a threat to the colony's stability and a breach of the Joint Declaration's pledge to maintain Hong Kong's existing systems. Moreover, PRC officials perceive rapid political liberalization as an infringement on their sovereignty, arguing that the British are trying to influence the structure of the SAR's post–1997 government.

The Chinese have claimed the right to speak out on such issues, insisting that their involvement does not constitute meddling in Hong Kong affairs. For example, PRC officials were widely reported to have pushed the Hong Kong government toward taking a neutral stance, rather than recommending further reform, in a 1987 Green Paper on representative government. The PRC has established "convergence" as the standard by which it will judge Hong Kong's political developments, insisting that reforms before 1997 must "converge" with the political structure outlined in the Basic Law to allow a smooth transition. The British administration in Hong Kong, which also has a diplomatic stake in the smooth transfer of authority, has been sensitive to Chinese concerns and has moved slowly toward democratization.

The greatest threat to Beijing's plans for a smooth transition comes from Hong Kong's students and liberal groups, a vocal minority that will continue to call for more rapid democratization than either the Hong Kong or PRC governments are willing to provide. While demands for representative government emerged in the late 1960s and began to bear fruit in the 1970s, liberal groups became far more aggressive following the signing of the Sino-British agreement and particulary during the drafting of the Basic Law. Following the crackdown on student demonstrators in the mainland in 1989, support for liberal initiatives grew significantly. Shocked by the massacre and frustrated by the fact that they have been locked out of crucial decisions over their own futures, Hong Kong's liberals will continue to voice their demands as 1997 approaches.

The basic elements of Beijing's response to the political reform question have become apparent in the course of this debate. Chinese officials will continue a public campaign of warning against "excessive" changes in Hong Kong's existing political structure, reasserting their right to determine the SAR's political system after 1997 and insisting that rapid changes would pose an unacceptable risk to the territory's stability. They will also continue to pressure the Hong Kong government to allow only gradual reforms, pointing out that a smooth transition is in the best interests of all parties. Finally, they will counter liberal demands by appealing to Hong Kong's large number of conservative industrialists, businessmen and professionals, who also tremble at the prospect of economic instability.

Still, there are no indications that PRC officials wish to interfere in Hong Kong's internal affairs before 1997 as long as a smooth transition remains likely. On policy matters not related to post–1997 arrangements, they will probably withhold judgement and cooperate with the Hong Kong government. One historically interesting example of this attitude was the Chinese expression of support for the Hong Kong Government's decision in 1987 to tear down a long-standing object of dispute, the Kowloon Walled City, and build a public park in its place. "An actual improvement of the living environment of the Kowloon Walled City not only accords with the vital interests of the inhabitants within the Kowloon Walled City but also with the interests of the Hong Kong inhabitants as a whole," an official statement explained.[7] Ultimately what Beijing hopes for is a minimum of disruption during the transition period. Given the atmosphere in the colony, however, at least some disruption in the form of more public protest is likely, and Beijing will be challenged to respond to those circumstances without contributing to instability.

Beyond 1997

The disputes that have accompanied the Basic Law drafting process are indicative of the challenges that PRC policy makers will face after 1997, though without the luxury of deferring the responsibility to Great Britain. There will be pressure for political change from within the SAR and internal competition for power that may become "adversarial" and therefore, from Beijing's perspective, undesirable. There will be policy disagreements within Hong Kong and between Hong Kong and Beijing. Hong Kong residents in the past decade have become more accustomed to making demands of their political leaders, and PRC officials will have to be prepared to respond to demands from the SAR. Their record so far has been mixed. Public concern in Hong Kong over the safety of the Daya Bay nuclear power plant, for example, led the Chinese government to establish a committee to consider safety issues concerning the plant. However, the attempt by several prominent Hong Kong residents to bring a petition to Beijing requesting the release of political prisoners was handled clumsily. The petition was confiscated, one member of the group was denied entry to China and the remaining members were put under heavy surveillance during their visit.

The PRC government will also be forced to resolve the difficult problem of integrating Hong Kong into the mainland. "One country, two systems" may be difficult to implement on several levels. In theoretical terms, it creates an awkward alliance between socialist and capitalist systems. The Chinese have justified this by arguing that pockets of capitalism may be used to contribute to socialist modernization, and by pointing to the Hong Kong agreement as a peaceful solution to the imperative of national reunification. Still, Deng Xiaoping has found it necessary to reiterate that the adoption of "one country, two systems" does not weaken the fundamental dominance of socialism in China, and other leaders may have to defend the policy on similar grounds in the future.

The question of administrative integration presents the greatest range of practical difficulties and therefore has been at the center of attention. Hong Kong after 1997 will be held responsible to Beijing on certain crucial matters but will enjoy far greater autonomy than any subnational unit in China, including the Special Economic Zones. The difficult problem for the central government will be to resist treating Hong Kong like another province. As years pass, officials in Beijing may be tempted to "run" Hong Kong, particularly if the local government experiences economic or political difficulties. Mechanisms for interference in Hong Kong's internal affairs are available, and the extent to which the central government will take advantage of them remains to be seen.

A great deal of effort, particularly in the JLG, has been devoted to the problem of economic integration. Arrangements have been made for Hong Kong's continued participation in a wide variety of international organizations and trade agreements so that, for most purposes, Hong Kong can be dealt with as a separate trading territory after 1997. The central government will continue to invest heavily in Hong Kong real estate and manufacturing in the years before 1997 to help maintain confidence there and because its investments have been profitable. After the transition, however, Beijing will have to be careful to avoid expecting too much from the SAR. For example, local investors will be very sensitive, as they have been in the past, to any business deals in Hong Kong that appear to grant special advantages to mainland firms. And the central government will have to accept normal downturns in Hong Kong's economy without moving to intervene.

The central government also faces the challenge of integrating Hong Kong's 5.6 million residents with the mainland's 1.1 billion, whose average standard of living is well below Hong Kong's. Xu Jiatun has stated that it will be necessary to educate the PRC's population about Hong Kong and the meaning of "one country, two systems." This will be especially important in Guangdong, where residents are better off than most other places in China, but where they are acutely aware of how far behind Hong Kong they remain.

The PRC's historical relationship with British Hong Kong indicates its capacity for dealing delicately with the territory, respecting the colony's unusual status while taking advantage of the benefits it offers. But Chinese officials have also made mistakes and have at times demonstrated a lack of understanding and tolerance for Hong Kong's way of life. After 1997, every action they take will be scrutinized carefully in Hong Kong, London and elsewhere to see if "one country, two systems," and "Hong Kong people ruling Hong Kong" can resolve the tension between national sovereignty and local autonomy. Chinese officials appear sincere in their desire to see Hong Kong continue to prosper as an SAR. But the results of the experiment on which they have embarked will be influenced by more than good intentions and therefore are difficult to predict.

Both the PRC and Hong Kong are currently undergoing dramatic and rapid change. To the extent that Chinese leaders hope to inherit the "status quo" in Hong Kong in 1997, they will be disappointed. Rather, the real test of Chinese policy will be whether the Joint Declaration and Basic Law will stand up under changing political and economic conditions. This will require considerable flexibility and a willingness to compromise as the "Hong Kong question" continues to dominate the Beijing–Hong Kong relationship well into the next century. The Chinese have demonstrated such a capacity for compromise throughout the history of their policy toward Hong Kong. In the future, the challenges of that policy, and the potential costs of its failure, will be greater than ever.

Notes

1. For a discussion of the different arguments attributed to "optimists" and "pessimists," see George L. Hicks, "Hong Kong on the Eve of Communist Rule," in Hungdah Chiu, Y. C. Jao and Yuan-li Wu, eds., *The Future of Hong Kong: Toward 1997 and Beyond* (N.Y.: Quorum Books, 1987): 23–55.

2. There were two major factors operating against such an approach on Thatcher's part. One was that Thatcher's visit to Beijing came on the heels of the Falklands War, in which Thatcher felt her hard-line position had been vindicated. The second was the possibility that a preemptive concession of sovereignty might leave Britain more vulnerable to other claims, such as over Gibraltar, in the future.

3. Gary Catron, *China and Hong Kong, 1945–1967* (Ph.D. Dissertation, Harvard University, 1971): 12.

4. *Hsin Wan Pao*, April 4, 1985, in Foreign Broadcast Information Service (FBIS), *Daily Report: China*, April 4, 1985, W5.

5. *Zhongguo Fazhi Bao* [China Legal News], Jan. 25, 1983, in FBIS, Feb. 1, 1985, E3.

6. *Hong Kong Standard*, Jan. 27, 1987, in FBIS, Jan. 14, 1987, W3.

7. *New China News Agency*, Jan. 14, 1987, in FBIS, Jan. 14, 1987, W3.

Bibliography

Arrangements for Testing the Acceptability in Hong Kong of the Draft Agreement on the Future of the Territory. Hong Kong: Government Printer, November 29, 1984.

Asia Yearbook. Hong Kong: Far Eastern Economic Review Ltd., 1973–.

Ayers, William. "The Hong Kong Strikes, 1920–1926." *Harvard Papers on China* 4 (1950): 94–130.

The Basic Law of the Hong Kong Special Administrative Region of China (Draft). April 1988 and February 1989.

Benton, Gregor. *The Hong Kong Crisis.* London: Pluto Press Ltd., 1983.

Birch, Alan. "Hong Kong in the Balance—August–September, 1945." Working Paper No. CC16, Contemporary Chinese Studies Programme, University of Hong Kong, 1981.

Bonavia, David. *Hong Kong 1997.* Hong Kong: South China Morning Post, 1983.

Bray, Dennis L. "Hong Kong: Its Economic Structure and Relationship with China." *Asian Affairs* 11 (Oct. 1980): 293–300.

Bucknall, Kevin B. "Hong Kong and China: The Present and Future Relationship." *Asia Pacific Community* 18 (Fall 1982): 106–28.

Catron, Gary. *China and Hong Kong, 1945–1967.* Ph.D. Dissertation, Harvard University, 1971.

_____ . "Hong Kong and Chinese Foreign Policy, 1955–1960." *China Quarterly* 51 (July–Sept. 1972): 405–24.

Chan, Lau Kit-Ching. "The Hong Kong Question during the Pacific War (1941–1945)." *The Journal of Imperial and Commonwealth History* 3, no. 1 (Oct. 1973): 56–78.

_____ . "The United States and the Question of Hong Kong, 1941–1945." *Journal of the Hong Kong Branch of the Royal Asiatic Society* 19 (1979): 1–20.

Chan, Ming K. *Labour and Empire: The Chinese Labour Movement in the Canton Delta, 1895–1927.* Ph.D. Dissertation, Stanford University, 1975.

Chen, Lung-Fong. *State Succession Relating to Unequal Treaties.* Hamden, Conn.: Archon Books, 1974.

Cheng, Joseph Y. S. "China's Foreign Policy: Continuity and Change," part 2. *Asian Quarterly* 1 (1977): 17–40.

_____ . "China's Foreign Policy After the Fall of the Gang of Four." *Asia Pacific Community* 10 (Fall 1980): 51–67.

_____ . "The Future of Hong Kong: A Hong Kong Belonger's View." *International Affairs* 58 (Summer 1982): 476–88.

_____, ed. *Hong Kong in Search of a Future.* Hong Kong: Oxford University Press, 1984.

_____, ed. *Hong Kong in Transition.* Hong Kong: Oxford University Press, 1986.

_____. "Hong Kong: The Pressure to Converge." *International Affairs,* 63 (Spring 1987): 271–83.

Chesneaux, Jean. *The Chinese Labor Movement, 1919–1927.* Stanford: Stanford University Press, 1968.

Chiang Kai-shek. *China's Destiny,* Wang Chung-hui, trans. N.Y.: De Capo Press, 1976.

Chinese Ministry of Information. *The Collected Wartime Messages of Generalissimo Chiang Kai-shek, 1937–1945.* 2 vols. N.Y.: John Day Co., 1946.

Ching, Frank. *Hong Kong and China: For Better or For Worse.* N.Y.: Foreign Policy Association, 1985.

Chiu, Hungdah. *The People's Republic of China and the Law of Treaties.* Cambridge: Harvard University Press, 1972.

Chiu, Hungdah, Y. C. Jao, and Yuan-li Wu, eds. *The Future of Hong Kong: Toward 1997 and Beyond.* N.Y.: Quorum Books, 1987.

Chou, David Shieu. *China and UN Decolonization.* Ph.D. Dissertation, Duke University, 1973.

Christie, Clive John. *The Problem of China in British Foreign Policy.* Ph.D. Dissertation, Cambridge University, St. John's College, 1971.

Chung, Rosemarie Lu Cee. *A Study of the 1925–26 Canton Strike-Boycott.* M.A. Thesis, University of Hong Kong, 1969.

Cohen, Jerome Alan, ed. *China's Practice of International Law: Some Case Studies.* Cambridge: Harvard University Press, 1972.

Cohen, Jerome Alan, and Hungdah Chiu. *People's China and International Law: A Documentary Study.* Princeton: Princeton University Press, 1974.

Committee of Hong Kong–Kowloon Chinese Compatriots for the Struggle Against Persecution by the British Authorities in Hong Kong. *The May Upheaval in Hong Kong.* Hong Kong, 1967.

Cooper, John. *Colony in Conflict: The Hong Kong Disturbances, May 1967–January 1968.* Hong Kong: Swindon Book Co., 1970.

David, Arie E. *The Strategy of Treaty Termination: Lawful Breaches and Retaliations.* London: Yale University Press, 1975.

Dicks, Anthony. "Treaty, Grant, Usage or Sufferance? Some Legal Aspects of the Status of Hong Kong." *China Quarterly* 95 (Sept. 1983): 427–55.

Doolin, Dennis J. *Territorial Claims in the Sino-Soviet Conflict.* Stanford: Stanford University Press, 1965.

Domes, Jürgen and Yu-ming Shaw, eds. *Hong Kong: A Chinese and International Concern.* Boulder, Colo.: Westview Press, 1988.

A Draft Agreement between the Government of the United Kingdom and Northern Ireland and the Government of the People's Republic of China on the Future of Hong Kong. Hong Kong: Government Printer, September 26, 1984.

Endacott, G. B. *A History of Hong Kong.* 2nd ed. Hong Kong: Oxford University Press, 1977.

_____. *Hong Kong Eclipse.* Edited and with additional material by Alan P. Birch. Hong Kong: Oxford University Press, 1978.

Endicott, Stephen Lyon. *Diplomacy and Enterprise: British China Policy, 1933–1937.* Vancouver: University of British Columbia, 1975.

Fairbank, John King, Edwin O. Reischauer, and Albert M. Craig. *East Asia: The Modern Transformation.* Tokyo: Charles E. Tuttle Co., 1965.

Far Eastern Economic Review. Hong Kong.

Far Eastern Economic Review Yearbook. Hong Kong: Far Eastern Economic Review Ltd., 1962–1972.

Fay, Peter Ward. *The Opium War, 1840–1842.* Chapel Hill: University of North Carolina Press, 1975.

Feuerwerker, Albert. "Chinese History and the Foreign Relations of Contemporary China." *The Annals of the American Academy of Political and Social Science* 402 (July 1972): 1–14.

Fingar, Thomas, ed. *China's Quest for Independence: Policy Evolution in the 1970s.* Boulder, Colo.: Westview Press, 1981.

Fishel, Wesley R. *The End of Extraterritoriality in China.* N.Y.: Octagon Books, 1974.

Foreign Relations of the United States. Annual. Washington, D.C.: U.S. Government Printing Press.

Friedman, Irving S. *British Relations with China, 1931–1939.* N.Y.: Institute of Pacific Relations, 1940.

Gernet, Jacques. *A History of Chinese Civilization.* Cambridge: Cambridge University Press, 1982.

Gleason, Gene. *Hong Kong.* London: Robert Hale Ltd., 1963.

Gray, Jack, and Gordon White, eds. *China's New Development Strategy.* London: Academic Press, 1982.

Green Paper: The Further Development of Representative Government in Hong Kong. Hong Kong: Government Printer, July 1984.

Green Paper: The 1987 Review of Developments in Representative Government. Hong Kong: Government Printer, May 1987.

Groves, R. G. "Militia, Market and Lineage: Chinese Resistance to the Occupation of Hong Kong's New Territories in 1899." *Journal of the Hong Kong Branch of the Royal Asiatic Society* 9 (1960): 31–64.

Gurtov, Melvin, and Byong-Moo Hwang. *China Under Threat: The Politics of Strategy and Diplomacy.* Baltimore: Johns Hopkins University Press, 1980.

Harris, P. B. "The International Future of Hong Kong." *International Affairs* 1 (Jan. 1972): 60–71.

Hinton, Harold C. *China's Turbulent Quest: An Analysis of China's Foreign Relations Since 1949.* Bloomington, Ind.: Indiana University Press, 1972.

———, ed. *The People's Republic of China, 1949–1979: A Documentary Survey.* Wilmington, Del.: Scholarly Resources, Inc., 1980.

Hong Kong Government Information Services Department. *Events in Hong Kong—1967: An Official Report.* Hong Kong: Government Printer, 1968.

"Hong Kong Original Correspondence." *Great Britain Colonial Office Papers.*

Howe, Christopher. "Growth, Public Policy and Hong Kong's Economic Relationship with China." *China Quarterly* 95 (Sept. 1983): 512–33.

Hsia, Ching-lin. *Studies in Chinese Diplomatic History.* Shanghai: Commercial Press, 1925.

Hsiung, James Chieh. *Law and Policy in China's Foreign Relations: A Study of Attitudes and Practice.* N.Y.: Columbia University Press, 1972.

Hsiung, James Chieh, and Samuel S. Kim, eds. *China in the Global Community.* N.Y.: Praeger Publishers, 1980.

Jain, J. P. *China in World Politics: A Study of Sino-British Relations, 1949–1975.* New Delhi: Radiant Publishers, 1976.

Jao, Y. C., Leung Chi-keung, Peter Wesley-Smith, and Wong Siu-lum, eds. *Hong Kong and 1997: Strategies for the Future.* Hong Kong: Centre for Asian Studies, University of Hong Kong, 1985.

Johnson, Chalmers. "The Mouse-Trapping of Hong Kong: A Game in Which Nobody Wins." *Issues and Studies* 20, no. 8 (Aug. 1984): 26–50.

Johnson, Graham E. "1997 and After: Will Hong Kong Survive? A Personal View." *Pacific Affairs* 59, no. 2 (Summer 1986): 237–54.

Keeton, G. W. *The Development of Extraterritoriality in China.* 2 vols. N.Y.: Howard Fertig, 1969.

King, Wunsz. "The Lease Conventions Between China and the Foreign Powers: An Interpretation." *The Chinese Social and Political Science Review* 1, no. 4 (Dec. 1916): 24–36.

————. *Woodrow Wilson, Wellington Koo and the China Question at the Paris Peace Conference.* Leyden: A. W. Sythoff, 1959.

————. *China at the Washington Conference, 1921–1922.* N.Y.: St. John's University Press, 1963.

Kuo, Warren, ed. *Foreign Policy Speeches by Chinese Communist Leaders, 1963–1975.* Taipei: Institute of International Relations, 1976.

Lau Siu-kai. *Society and Politics in Hong Kong.* Hong Kong: The Chinese University Press, 1982.

Lau Siu-kai and Kuan Hsin-chi. "Hong Kong After the Sino-British Agreement: The Limits to Change." *Pacific Affairs* 59, no. 2 (Summer 1986): 214–36.

Lawrie, Gordon. "Hong Kong and the People's Republic of China: Past and Future." *International Affairs* 56 (Spring 1980): 280–95.

Liao, Kuang-sheng, ed. *Modernization and Diplomacy of China.* Hong Kong: The Chinese University Press, 1981.

————. *Antiforeignism and Modernization in China, 1860–1980: Linkage Between Domestic Politics and Foreign Policy.* Hong Kong: The Chinese University Press, 1984.

Louis, William Roger. *British Strategy in the Far East, 1919–1939.* London: Clarendon Press, 1971.

Luard, Evan. *Britain and China.* London: Chatto and Windus, 1962.

MacKinnon, Stephen R. *Power and Politics in Contemporary China: Yuan Shi-kai in Beijing and Tianjin, 1902–1908.* Berkeley: University of California Press, 1980.

MacMurray, John V. A., ed. *Treaties and Agreements With and Concerning China, 1894–1919.* N.Y.: Howard Fertig, 1973.

"Manifesto of the National People's Convention Concerning the Abrogation of Unequal Treaties." *The Chinese Social and Political Science Review,* vol. 15 supplement (1931–32): 461–65.

Millard, Thomas F. *The End of Extraterritoriality in China.* Shanghai: A. B. C. Press, 1931.

Miners, Norman. "Can the Colony of Hong Kong Survive 1997?" *Asia Pacific Community* 6 (Fall 1979): 100–114.

_____. *The Government and Politics of Hong Kong.* Hong Kong: Oxford University Press, 1981.

_____. *Hong Kong under Imperial Rule, 1912–1941.* Hong Kong: Oxford University Press, 1987.

Morris, Jan. *Hong Kong.* N.Y.: Random House, 1988.

Motz, Earl John. *Great Britain, Hong Kong and Canton: The Canton–Hong Kong Strike and Boycott of 1925–1926.* Ph.D. Dissertation, Michigan State University, 1972.

Nozari, Fariborz. *Unequal Treaties in International Law.* Stockholm: S. Byran Sundt and Co., 1971.

Overholt, William H. "Hong Kong and the Crisis of Sovereignty." *Asian Survey* 24, no. 24 (April 1984): 471–84.

_____. "Hong Kong After the Chinese-British Agreement." *Asian Perspective* 9, no. 2 (Fall–Winter 1985): 257–73.

"The Peace Conference: Questions for Readjustment." *The Chinese Social and Political Science Review* 5, nos. 1–2 (March–June 1920): 115–61.

Pollack, Jonathan D. *Security, Strategy, and the Logic of Chinese Foreign Policy.* Berkeley: Institute of East Asian Studies, University of California, 1981.

Porter, Brian. *Britain and the Rise of Communist China.* London: Oxford University Press, 1967.

Pye, Lucian. "The International Position of Hong Kong." *China Quarterly* 95 (Sept. 1983): 456–68.

Rabushka, Alvin. *Hong Kong: A Study in Economic Freedom.* Chicago: University of Chicago Press, 1979.

Remer, C. F., with William B. Palmer. *A Study of Chinese Boycotts.* Baltimore: Johns Hopkins Press, 1933.

"Report of the Commission on Extraterritoriality in China," Sept. 16, 1926. Washington, D.C.: Government Printing Office, 1926.

Roots, John McCook. *Chou.* N.Y.: Doubleday and Co., 1978.

Rowe, David Nelson. *China Among the Powers.* N.Y.: Harcourt, Brace and Co., 1945.

Sayle, Murray. "Red Flags, Running Dogs and Air Conditioned Horses." *New Statesman* 95 (May 9, 1975): 202–3.

Scobell, Andrew. "Hong Kong's Influence on China: The Tail that Wags the Dog?" *Asian Survey* 28, no. 6 (June 1988): 599–612.

Scott, Gary L. *Chinese Treaties: The Post-Revolutionary Restoration of International Law and Order.* Dobbs Ferry, N.Y.: Oceana Publications, 1975.

Selected Works of Mao Tse-tung. Beijing: Foreign Languages Press, 1965.

Sharman, Lyon. *Sun Yat-sen: His Life and its Meaning.* Stanford: Stanford University Press, 1934.

Shieh, Milton J. T. *The Kuomintang: Selected Historical Documents, 1894–1969.* N.Y.: St. John's University Press, 1970.

South China Morning Post. Hong Kong.

A Statement of the Views of the Chinese Government on the Report of the Commission of Enquiry. N.Y.: The China Institute in America, 1932.

Sutter, Robert G. *Chinese Foreign Policy After the Cultural Revolution.* Boulder, Colo.: Westview Press, 1978.

Teng, Ssu-yu, and John King Fairbank. *China's Response to the West.* Cambridge: Harvard University Press, 1954.

Tongxiang 1997: Xianggang Qiantu Wenti Zhuanji [Onward to 1997: Special Volume on the Question of Hong Kong's Future]. Hong Kong: Mirror Cultural Enterprises Ltd., 1983.

Tung, William L. *China and Some Phases of International Law.* London: Oxford University Press, 1940.

_____. *China and the Foreign Powers: The Impact of and Reaction to Unequal Treaties.* Dobbs Ferry, N.Y.: Oceana Publications, 1970.

_____. *V. K. Wellington Koo and China's Wartime Diplomacy.* N.Y.: St. John's University Press, 1977.

Tyau, M. T. Z. "China and the Peace Conference." *The Chinese Social and Political Science Review* 2, no. 2 (June 1917): 22–54.

_____. "Diplomatic Relations Between China and the Powers Since, and Concerning, the European War." *The Chinese Social and Political Science Review* 2, no. 4 (Dec. 1917): 6–67.

Vincent, John Carter. *The Extraterritoriality System in China: Final Phase.* Cambridge: East Asian Research Center, Harvard University, 1970.

Wesley-Smith, Peter. "The Proposed Establishment of a 'China Office' in Hong Kong." *Journal of Oriental Studies* 19, no. 2 (1981): 175–84.

_____. *Unequal Treaty, 1898–1997: China, Great Britain and Hong Kong's New Territories.* Hong Kong: Oxford University Press, 1983.

Wesley-Smith, Peter and Albert Chen, eds. *The Basic Law and Hong Kong's Future.* Hong Kong: Butterworths, 1988.

White Paper: The Development of Representative Government: The Way Forward. Hong Kong: Government Printer, February 1988.

White Paper: The Further Development of Representative Government in Hong Kong. Hong Kong: Government Printer, November 1984.

White Paper on the Draft Hong Kong (British Nationality) Order 1986. Hong Kong: Government Printer, October 17, 1985.

Willoughby, Westel W. *China at the Conference: A Report.* Baltimore: Johns Hopkins Press, 1922.

_____. *Foreign Rights and Interests in China.* Orig. pub. 1927. Taipei: Ch'eng Wen Publishing Co., 1966.

Wilson, Dick. "New Thoughts on the Future of Hong Kong." *Pacific Community* 8, no. 4 (July 1977): 588–99.

Woodhead, H. G. W. "Shanghai and Hong Kong: A British View." *Foreign Affairs* 23 (Jan. 1945): 295–307.

Wu, Chun-hsi. *Dollars, Dependents and Dogma: Overseas Chinese Remittances to Communist China.* Stanford: The Hoover Institution, 1967.

Wu, Yuan-li. "The Future of Hong Kong Before and After 1997." *American-Asian Review* 2, no. 4 (Winter 1984): 13–23.

Xianggang yu Zhongguo: Lishi Wenxian Ziliao Huibian [Hong Kong and China: A Compilation of Historical Documents and Materials]. Hong Kong: Wide Angle Press, 1981.

Xianggang Luxiang [Hong Kong's Road Ahead]. Hong Kong: Pai Hsing Press, 1983.

Xue Fengxuan, ed. *Zhonggang Jingji yu Xianggang Qiantu* [China–Hong Kong Economics and the Future of Hong Kong]. Hong Kong: Wide Angle Press, 1982.

Yahuda, Michael B. *China's Role in World Affairs.* London: Croom Helm, 1978.

Young, Ernest B. *The Presidency of Yuan Shih-kai: Liberalism and Dictatorship in Early Republican China.* Ann Arbor: University of Michigan Press, 1977.

Young, John. "China's Role in Two Hong Kong Disturbances: A Scenario for the Future?" *Journal of Oriental Studies* 19, no. 2 (1981): 158–74.

_____. "Face and Peking's Stand on Treaties." *South China Morning Post*, June 13, 1983, 2.

Youngson, A. J. *Hong Kong: Economic Growth and Policy.* Hong Kong: Oxford University Press, 1982.

_____, ed. *China and Hong Kong: The Economic Nexus.* Hong Kong: Oxford University Press, 1983.

Index